The Wisdom of James Allen II

- Light on Life's Difficulties
- Above Life's Turmoil
- The Life Triumphant

The Wisdom of James Allen II

Three Classic Works from the author of *As a Man Thinketh*

- Light on Life's Difficulties
- Above Life's Turmoil
- The Life Triumphant

Laurel Creek Press
San Diego, California 2003

Laurel Creek Press is an imprint of Blue Dove Press—A project of the Blue Dove Foundation, an independent, nonprofit organization dedicated to making available the finest spiritual books and works from the world's religious and wisdom traditions.
For a free catalog contact:
The Blue Dove Foundation,
P.O. Box 261611, San Diego, CA 92196
858-623-3330 or 800-691-1008
www.laurelcreekpress.com or www.bluedove.org

8 7 6 5 4 3 2 1

The Wisdom of James Allen II

Edited by Andy Zubko. This book contains the complete and unabridged text of each of the three listed works. For clarity, some obscure or archaic English words and phrases were rendered into modern usage. James Allen used the generic masculine in his writings, as was the common practice of his time. This was retained in order to remain true to his voice.

Cover and Text Design: Brian Moucka.
Special thanks to Beth Kleinman for her dedicated efforts in the production of this book

Library of Congress Cataloging-in-Publication Data

Allen, James, 1864-1912

The wisdom of James Allen II : Laurel Creek James Allen wisdom series / James Allen

p. cm.

ISBN 1-889606-07-3 (perfect bound)

1. New Thought. I. Title

BF639 .A672 2000
289.9'8--dc21 00-061207
CIP

About James Allen

JAMES ALLEN has been called the "literary mystery man" of the twentieth century. Although his best-selling classic *As a Man Thinketh* has inspired millions around the world, little is known about the author himself.

What is known about James Allen is that he was born in 1864 in Leicester, England. His father was a well-to-do businessman who, because of poor economic conditions, went bankrupt in 1878 and was tragically murdered one year later. This required James to leave school at the age of fifteen to help support his family. James eventually married and became a personal secretary for an executive of a large English corporation.

At the age of 38, James Allen reached what can

be called a crossroads in his life. Influenced by the writings of Leo Tolstoy, James came to the realization that a life devoted to making money and spending it on frivolous activities was a meaningless way to live. He retired from his employment and moved with his wife to a small cottage on the southwest shore of England to pursue a life of contemplation. It was here at Iltracombe that James pursued his dream of voluntary poverty, spiritual self-discipline, and a life of simplicity as taught by his mentor, Tolstoy.

A typical James Allen day would be to rise very early in the morning and walk to a bluff overlooking the ocean, where he would remain in meditation for an hour or so. And as the cobwebs which had obscured his spiritual vision lifted, the secrets of the universe would unfold before him. Quietly these impressions would be recorded within. Afterwards, he would return home and pen his insights on paper. Afternoons were committed to tending his garden; evenings to communion with townsfolk who wished to discuss loftier philosophical issues.

For ten years James Allen led this quiet, pensive life, earning a small stipend from royalties paid on his writing. Then suddenly, at the age of 48, he passed away. He died the way he lived, a virtual unknown, untouched by fame, unrewarded by fortune. It would only be after his death that the reading public would come to recognize the genius and inspiration of his work. But this is the way the anonymous English mystic would have wanted it—to posthumously share his spiritual insights with the world.

James Allen's classic work, *As a Man Thinketh*, as well as *The Path to Prosperity*, *The Way of Peace*, *The Mastery of Destiny* and *Entering the Kingdom* have all been combined in the first volume of this set, *The Wisdom of James Allen*.

In this second volume, *The Wisdom of James Allen II*, we have compiled three more of James Allen's classic works: *Light on Life's Difficulties*, *Above Life's Turmoil*, and *The Life Triumphant*. These books are his loving bequest to the world.

Foreword

I LOOKED AROUND UPON THE WORLD, and saw that it was shadowed by sorrow and scorched by the fierce fires of suffering. And I looked for the cause. I looked around, but I could not find it; I looked in books, but I could not find it; I looked within, and found there both the cause and the self-made nature of that cause. I looked again, and deeper, and found the remedy. I found one Law, the Law of Love; one Life, the life of adjustment to that Law; one Truth, the Truth of a conquered mind and a quiet and obedient heart.

And I dreamed of writing books which would help men and women, whether rich or poor, learned or unlearned, worldly or unworldly to find within themselves the source of all success, all happiness, all accomplishment, all truth. And the dream remained with me, and at last became substantial; and now I send forth these books into the world on a mission of healing and blessedness, knowing that they cannot fail to reach the homes and hearts of those who are waiting and ready to receive them.

James Allen

CONTENTS:

The Wisdom of James Allen II

- Light on Life's Difficulties
- Above Life's Turmoil
- The Life Triumphant

I, Truth, am thy Redeemer, come to Me;
Lay down thy sin and pain and wild unrest;
And I will calm thy spirit's stormy sea,
Pouring the oil of peace upon thy breast:
Friendless and lone—lo, I abide with thee.

Defeated and deserted, cast away,
What refuge hast thou? Whither canst thou fly?
Upon my changeless breast thy burdens lay;
I am thy certain refuge, even I:
All things are passing; I alone can stay.

Lo I, the Great Forsaken, am the Friend
Of the forsaken; I, whom man despise,
The Weak, the helpless, and despised defend;
I gladden aching hearts and weeping eyes;
Rest thou in Me, I am thy sorrow's end.

Lover, friends and wealth, pleasure and fame—
These fail and change, and pass into decay;
I blame thee not, nor turn my face away:
In My calm bosom hide thy sin and shame.

Book One

Light on Life's Difficulties

Light on Life's Difficulties

Table of Contents

Foreword

WHEN A MAN enters a dark room he is not sure of his movements, he cannot see objects around him, or properly locate them, and is liable to hurt himself by coming into sudden contact with them. But let a light be introduced, and immediately all confusion disappears. Every object is seen, and there is no danger of being hurt.

To the majority, life is such a dark room, and their frequent hurts—their disappointments, perplexities, sorrows and pains—are caused by sudden contact with principles which they do not see, and are therefore not prepared to deal with. But when the light of wisdom is introduced into the darkened understanding, confusion vanishes, difficulties are dissolved, all things are seen in their true place and proportion, and henceforth the man walks open-eyed and unhurt, in the clear light of wise comprehension.

—James Allen

The Light That Leads to Perfect Peace

THIS BOOK IS INTENDED to be a strong and kindly companion, as well as a source of spiritual renewal and inspiration to those who aim at a life well-lived and made strong and serene. It will help its readers to transform themselves into the ideal character they would wish to be, and to make their life here that blessed thing which the majority only hope for in some future life.

Our life is what we make it by our own thoughts and deeds. It is our own state and attitude of mind which determine whether we are happy or unhappy, strong or weak, sinful or holy, foolish or wise. If one is unhappy, that state of mind belongs to himself, and is originated within himself. It is a state which responds to certain outward happenings, but its cause lies within and not in those outward occurrences. If one is weak in will, he has brought himself to, and remains in, that condition by the course of thought and action which he has chosen and is still choosing. If one is sinful, it is because he has committed, and continues to commit, sinful acts. If he is foolish, it is because he himself does foolish things.

A man has no character, no soul, no life apart from his thoughts and deeds. What they are, that he is. As they are modified, so does he change. He is endowed with will, and can modify his character. As the carpenter changes the block of wood into a beautiful piece of furniture, so can the erring and sin-stricken man change himself into a wise and truth-loving being.

Each man is responsible for the thoughts which he thinks and the acts which he does, for his state of mind, and the life which he lives. No power, no event, no circumstance can compel a man to evil and unhappiness. He himself is his own compeller. He thinks and acts by his own volition. No being, however wise and great—even the Supreme—can make him good and happy. He himself must choose the good, and thereby find the happy.

And because of this—that when a man wishes and wills he can find the Good and the True, and enjoy its bliss and peace—there is eternal gladness in the Courts of Truth, and holy joy among the Perfect Ones.

The Gates of Heaven Are Open

The Gates of Heaven are forever open, and no one is prevented from entering by any will or power but his own. But no one can enter the Kingdom of Heaven so long as he is enamored of, and chooses, the seductions of hell, so long as he resigns himself to sin and sorrow.

There is a larger, higher, nobler, diviner life than that of sinning and suffering, which is so common—in which, indeed, nearly all are immersed—a life of victory over sin, and triumph over evil; a life wise and happy, kind and tranquil, virtuous and peaceful. This life can be found and lived now, and he who lives it is steadfast in the midst of change; restful among the restless; peaceful, though surrounded by strife. Should death confront him, he is calm. Though assailed by persecution, he knows no bitterness, and his heart is compassionate and filled with rejoicing. In this supremely beautiful life there is no evil, sin and sorrow are ended, and aching hearts and weeping eyes are no more.

The life of triumph is not for those who are satisfied with any lower conditions. It is for those who thirst for it and are willing to achieve it; who are eager for righteousness as the miser is for gold. It is always at hand, and is offered to all, and blessed are they who accept and embrace it. They will enter the World of Truth; they will find the Perfect Peace.

Light on Facts and Hypotheses

When freedom of thought and freedom of expression abound, there is much controversy and much confusion. Yet it is from such controversial confusion that the simple facts of life emerge, attracting us with their eternal uniformity and harmony, and appealing forcibly to us with their invisible simplicity and truth.

We are living in an age of freedom and mental conflict. Never were religious sects so numerous. Schools—philosophical, occult, and otherwise—abound, and each is eager for the perpetuation and dominance of its own explanation of the universe. The world is in a condition of mental ferment. Contradiction has reached the point of confusion, so that the earnest seeker for Truth can find no solid rock of refuge in the opposing systems which are presented to him. He is thereby thrown back upon himself, upon those incontrovertible facts of his own being which are ever with him—which are, indeed, himself, his life.

Facts Versus Hypotheses

Controversy is ranged around hypotheses, not around facts. Fact is fixed and final; hypothesis is variable and vanishing. In his present stage of development, man is not alive to the beautiful simplicity of facts, nor to the power of satisfaction which is inherent in them. He does not perceive the intrinsic loveliness of truth, but must add something to it. Hence, when fact is named, the question almost invariably arises, "How can you explain the fact?" and then follows a hypothesis which leads to another hypothesis, and so on and on until the fact is altogether lost sight of amid a mass of contradictory suppositions. Thus arise the sects and controversial schools.

The clear perception of one fact will lead to the perception of other facts, but a supposition, while appearing to elucidate a fact, does in reality cover it up. We cannot realize the stately splendor of Truth while playing with the gaudy and attractive toys of pretty hypotheses. Truth is not an opinion, nor can any opinion enlarge or adorn it. Fact and supposition are eternally separate, and the cleverest intellectual jugglery—while it may entertain and deceive even the elect—cannot in the slightest degree alter a fact or affect the nature of things-as-they-are. Because of this, the true teacher abandons the devious path of hypothesis, and deals only with the simple facts of life. He fixes the attention of men and women upon these, instead of increasing confusion and intensifying wordy warfare by foisting another assumption upon a world already lost and bewildered in a maze of hypotheses.

The facts of life are ever before us, and can be understood and known if we but abandon our egotism and the blinding delusions which that egotism creates. Man need not go beyond his own being to find wisdom, and the facts of that being afford a sufficient basis on which to erect a temple of knowledge of such beauty and dimensions that it shall at once emancipate and glorify.

You Are Not Separate from Mind

Man is; and as he thinks, so he is. A perception and realization of these two facts alone—of man's being and thinking—lead into a vast avenue of knowledge which cannot stop short of the highest wisdom and perfection. One of the reasons why men do not become wise is that they occupy themselves with interminable speculations about a soul separate from themselves—that is, from their own mind—and so blind themselves to their actual nature and being. The supposition of a separate soul veils the eyes of man so that he does not see himself, does not know his mentality, is unaware of the nature of his thoughts without which he would have no conscious life.

Man's life is actual; his thoughts are actual; his life is actual. To occupy ourselves with the investigation of things that are is the way of wisdom. Man considered as above, beyond, and separate from mind and thought, is speculative and not actual, and to occupy ourselves with the study of things that are not, is the way of folly.

Man cannot be separated from his mind; his life cannot be separated from his thoughts. Mind, thought, and life are as inseparable as light, radiance, and color, and are no more in need of another factor to elucidate them than are light, radiance, and color. The facts are all-sufficient and contain within themselves the groundwork of all knowledge concerning them.

The Law of Change

Man as mind is subject to change. He is not something "made" and finally completed, but has within him the capacity for progress. By the universal law of evolution he has become what he is, and is becoming that which he will be. His being is modified by every thought he thinks. Every experience affects his character. Every effort he makes changes his mentality. Herein is the secret of man's degradation, and also of his power and salvation if he but utilize this law of change in the right choice of thought.

To live is to think and act, and to think and act is to change. While man is ignorant of the nature of thought, he continues to change for better and worse; but, being acquainted with the nature of thought, he intelligently accelerates and directs the process of change, and only for the better.

What the sum total of a man's thoughts are, that he is. From this sameness of thought with man there is not the slightest fractional deviation. There is a change as a result with the addition and subtraction of thought, but the mathematical law is an invariable quality.

Seeing that man is mind, that mind is composed of thought, and that thought is subject to change, it follows that deliberately to change the thought is to change the man.

Purification of the Heart

All religions work upon the heart, the thought of man, with the object of directing it into purer and higher channels. Success in this direction, whether partial or complete, is called "salvation"—that is, deliverance from one kind of thought, one condition of mind, by the substitution of another thought, another condition.

It is true that the dispensers of religion today do not know this because of the hypothetical veil which intervenes between the fact and their consciousness. But they do it without knowing it, and the Great Teachers who founded the various religions, built upon this fact, as their precepts plainly show. The chief things upon which these Teachers lay such stress, and so constantly reiterate—such as the purification of the heart, the thinking of right thoughts, and the doing of good deeds—what are they but calls to a higher, nobler mode of thought-energizing forces urging men and women to make an effort in the choosing of thoughts which shall lift them into realms of greater power, greater good, greater bliss?

Aspiration, meditation, devotion—these are the chief means which men in all ages employ to reach up to higher modes of thought, wider airs of peace, vaster realms of knowledge, for "as he thinketh in his heart, so is he." He is saved from himself—from his own folly and suffering—by creating within new habits of thoughts, by becoming a new thinker, a new man.

Should a man by a supreme effort succeed in thinking as Jesus thought—not by imitation, but by a sudden realization of his indwelling power—he would be as Jesus.

The Difference Between Great and Small

In the Buddhistic records there is an instance of a man, not the possessor of great piety or wisdom, who asked Buddha how one might attain the highest wisdom and enlightenment. Buddha replied, "By ceasing all desire." It is recorded that the man let go of all personal desires and at once realized the highest wisdom and enlightenment.

One of the sayings of Buddha runs, "The only miracle with which the wise man concerns himself is the transformation of a sinner into a saint." Emerson also referred to this transforming power of change of thought when he said: "It is as easy to be great as to be small," which is closely akin to that other great and oft-repeated but little understood saying: "Be ye therefore perfect, even as your Father which is in Heaven is perfect."

And, after all, what is the fundamental difference between a great man and a small one? It is one of thought, of mental attitude. True, it is one of knowledge, but then, knowledge cannot be separated from thought. Every substitution of a better for a worse thought is a transforming agency which marks an important advance in knowledge. Throughout the whole range of human life, from the lowest savage to the highest type of man, thought determines character, condition, knowledge.

The Sage, Master of Thought

The mass of humanity moves slowly along the evolutionary path urged by the blind impulse of its dominant thoughts as they are stimulated and called forth by external things. But the true thinker, the sage, travels swiftly and intelligently along a chosen path of his own. The multitudes, unenlightened concerning their spiritual nature, are the slaves of thought, but the sage is the master of thought. They follow blindly, he chooses intelligently. They obey the impulse of the moment, thinking of their immediate pleasure and happiness; he commands and subdues impulse, resting upon that which is permanently right. They, obeying blind impulse, violate the laws of righteousness; he, conquering impulse, obeys the law of righteousness. The sage stands face to face with the facts of life. He knows the nature of thought. He understands and obeys the law of his being.

But the sorrow-burdened victim of blind impulse can open his mental eyes and see the true nature of things when he wishes to do so. The sage—intelligent, radiant, calm—and the fool—confused, darkened, disturbed—are one in essence, and are divided only by the nature of their thoughts. When the fool turns away from and abandons his foolish thoughts and chooses and adopts wise thoughts, lo! he becomes a sage.

Choosing Wise Thoughts

Socrates saw the essential oneness of virtue and knowledge, and so every sage sees. Learning may aid and accompany wisdom, but it does not lead to it. Only the choosing of wise thoughts, and, necessarily, the doing of wise deeds, leads to wisdom. A man may be learned in the schools, but foolish in the school of life. Not the committing of words to memory, but the establishing of oneself in purer thoughts, nobler thinking, leads to the peace-giving revelations of true knowledge.

Folly and wisdom, ignorance and enlightenment, are not merely the result of thought, they are thought itself. Both cause and effect—effort and result—are contained in thought.

All that we are is the result of what we have thought.
It is founded on our thoughts;
it is made up of our thoughts.

Man is not a being possessing a soul. He himself is soul. He himself is the thinker and doer, actor and knower. His composite mentality is himself. His spiritual nature is rounded by his sphere of thought. He it is that desires and sorrows, enjoys and suffers, loves and hates. The mind is not the instrument of a metaphysical, superhuman soul. Man is soul; mind is being; mind is man.

Man can find himself. He can see himself as he is. When he is prepared to turn from the illusory and self-created world of hypothesis in which he wanders and to stand face to face with actuality, then will he know himself as he is. Moreover, he can picture himself as he would wish to be, and he can create within him the new thinker, the new man. For every moment is the time of choice—and every hour is destiny.

Light on the Law of Cause and Effect in Human Life

HOW FREQUENTLY PEOPLE associate the word "law" with hardness and cruelty! It seems to embody for them nothing but an inflexible tyranny. This arises partly from their inability to perceive principles apart from persons, and partly from the idea that the office of law is solely to punish. Viewed from such an attitude of mind, the term "law" is hazily regarded as some sort of indefinite personality whose business it is to hunt transgressors and crush them with overwhelming punishments.

Now while law punishes, its primary office is to protect. Even the laws which man makes are framed by him to protect himself from his own baser passions. The law of our country is instituted for the protection of life and property, and it only comes into operation as a punishing factor when it is violated. Offenders against it probably think of it as cruel, and doubtless regard it with terror, but to them that obey it, it is an abiding protector and friend, and can hold for them no terror.

So with the Divine Law which is the stay of the Universe, the heart and life of the Cosmos—it is that which protects and upholds, and it is no less protective in its penalties than in its peaceful blessings. It is, indeed, an eternal protection which is never for one moment withheld, and it shields all beings against themselves by bringing all violations of itself, whether ignorant or willful, through pain to nothingness.

The Law is Eternal Kindness

Law cannot be partial. It is an unvarying mode of action, disobeying which, we are hurt; obeying, we are made happy. Neither protection nor supplication can alter it, for if it could be altered or annulled the universe would collapse and chaos would prevail. It is not less kind that we should suffer the penalty of our wrongdoing than that we should enjoy the blessedness of our right-doing. If we could escape the effects of our ignorance and sin, all security would be gone, and there would be no refuge, for we could then be equally doubtful of the result of our wisdom and goodness. Such a scheme would be one of caprice and cruelty, whereas law is a method of justice and kindness.

Indeed, the supreme law is the principle of eternal kindness, faultless in working and infinite in application. It is none other than that:

Eternal Love, forever full,
Forever flowing free,

of which the Christian sings and the "Boundless Compassion" of Buddhistic precepts and poetry.

The law which punishes us is the law which preserves us. When in their ignorance men would destroy themselves, its everlasting arms are thrown about them in loving, albeit sometimes painful, protection. Every pain we suffer brings us nearer to the knowledge of the Divine Wisdom. Every blessing we enjoy speaks to us of the perfection of the Great Law, and of the fullness of bliss that shall be man's when he has come to his heritage of Divine Knowledge.

We progress by learning, and we learn, up to a certain point, by suffering. When the heart is mellowed by love, the law of love is perceived in all its wonderful kindness. When wisdom is acquired, peace is assured.

No One Can Adjust the Law

We cannot alter the law of things, which is of sublime perfection. But we can alter ourselves so as to comprehend more and more of that perfection and make its grandeur ours. To wish to bring down the perfect to the imperfect is the height of folly, but to strive to bring the imperfect up to the perfect is the height of wisdom.

Seers of the Cosmos do not mourn over the scheme of things. They see the universe as the perfect whole, not as an imperfect jumble of parts. The Great Teachers are men and women of abiding joy and heavenly peace.

The blind captive of unholy desire may cry:

Ah! Love: could you and I with him conspire
To grasp this sorry scheme of things entire,
Would we not shatter it to bits, and then
Remold it nearer to the heart's desire?

This is the wish of the carnal nature, the wish to enjoy unlawful pleasures to any extent, and not reap any painful consequences. It is such men who regard the universe as a "sorry scheme of things." They want the universe to bend to their will and desire; want lawlessness, not law.

But the wise man bends his will and subjects his desire to the Divine Order, and he sees the universe as the glorious perfection of an infinitude of parts.

Buddha always referred to the moral law of the universe as the Good Law, and indeed it is not rightly perceived if it is thought of as anything but good; for in it there can be no grain of evil, no element of kindness. It is no iron-hearted monster crushing the weak and destroying the ignorant, but a soothing love and brooding compassion shielding the tenderest from harm, and protecting the strongest from a too destructive use of their strength. It destroys all evil, it preserves all good. It enfolds the tiniest seedling in its care, and it destroys the most colossal wrong with a breath. To perceive it is the beatific vision. To know it is the beatific bliss; and they who perceive and know it are at peace. They are glad forevermore.

Such is the law which moves the righteousness,
Which none at last can turn aside or stay;
The heart of it is love; the end of it
Is peace and consummation sweet: obey.

Light on Values—Spiritual and Material

IT IS AN OLD-TIME AXIOM that "everything has its price." Everybody knows this commercially, but how few know it spiritually. Business consists of a mutual interchange of equitable values. The customer gives money and receives goods, and the merchant gives goods and receives money. This method is universal, and is regarded by all as just.

In spiritual things the method is the same, but the form of interchange is different. For material things a material thing is given in exchange. Now these two forms of exchange cannot be transposed; they are of reverse natures, and remain eternally separate. Thus a man may bring money to a shop and ask for food, or clothing, or literature, and he will receive goods to the value of his money. But if he were to take a dollar to a teacher of Truth, and ask to be supplied with a dollar's worth of religion, or righteousness, or wisdom, he would be told that those things cannot be purchased with money, that their spiritual nature excludes them from business transactions.

The wise teacher, however, would also tell him that these spiritual necessities must be purchased. Though money cannot buy them, they have their price, and something must be parted with before they can be received. In a word, instead of offering money he must offer up self, or selfishness. For so much selfishness given up, so much religion, righteousness, and wisdom would be immediately received, without fail, and with perfect equity. For if a man is sure of receiving perishable food and clothing for the money he puts down, how much more surely will he receive the imperishable spiritual sustenance and protection for the selfishness which he lays down! Shall the law operate in the lesser and fail in the greater? Man may fail to observe the law, but the law is infallible.

The Interchange of Material Goods:

A man may love his money, but he must part with it before he can receive the material comforts of life. Likewise, a man may love his selfish gratifications, but he must give them up before he can receive the spiritual comforts of religion.

Now when a tradesman gives goods for money, it is not that he may keep the money, but that he may give it in exchange for other goods. The primary function of business is not to enable everybody to hoard up money, but to facilitate the interchange of commodities. The miser is the greatest of all failures, and he may die of starvation and exposure while being a millionaire, because he is a worshipper of the letter of money, and an ignorer of its spirit—the spirit of mutual interchange.

Money is a means, not an end; its exchange is a sign that goods are being justly given and received. Thus commerce, with all its innumerable ramifications of detail, is reducible to one primary principle, namely: Mutual interchange of the material necessities of life.

The Interchange of Spiritual Goods

Now let us follow this principle into the spiritual sphere, and trace there its operation. When a spiritual man gives spiritual things—kindness, sympathy, love—and receives happiness in return, it is not that he may hoard and hug to himself that happiness, but that he may give it to others, and so receive back spiritual things. The primary function of spirituality is not to hoard up personal pleasure, but to render actual the interchange of spiritual blessings.

The most selfish man—he whose chief object is the getting of happiness for himself—is a spiritual miser. His mind may perish of spiritual destitution, though he be surrounded with the objects which he has obtained to pander to his pleasure, because he is worshipping the letter of happiness and is ignoring its spirit—the spirit of unselfish interchange. The object of selfishness is the getting of personal pleasure, or happiness; the object of religion is the defusion of virtue. Thus religion, with all its innumerable creeds, may be resolved into one primary principle, namely: Mutual interchange of spiritual blessings.

Bestowing Spiritual Blessings

What, then, are the spiritual blessings? They are kindness, brotherliness, goodwill, sympathy, forbearance, patience, trustfulness, peacefulness, love unending, and compassion unlimited. These blessings, these necessities for the starving spirit of man, can be obtained, but their price must be paid. Unkindness, uncharitableness, ill will, hardness, ill temper, impatience, suspicion, strife, hatred, and cruelty—all these, along with the happiness, the personal satisfaction, which they give, must be yielded up. These spiritual coins, dead in themselves, must be parted with, and when parted with, there will be immediately received their spiritual counterparts, the living and imperishable blessings to which they are a means and of which they are a sign.

To conclude, when a man gives money to a merchant and receives goods in return, he does not wish to have his money again. He has willingly parted with it forever and is satisfied with the exchange. So when a man gives up unrighteousness in exchange for righteousness, he does not wish to have his selfish pleasures back again. He has given them up forever, and is satisfied and at peace.

Thus also, when one bestows a gift, even though it be a material gift, he does not look for the receiver to send him back its value in money, because it is a spiritual deed and not a business transaction. The material thing thus represents the interchange of spiritual blessings, and its accompanying bliss, the bliss of a gift bestowed and that of a gift received.

~ Light on Life's Difficulties

Spiritual Things Cannot Be Bought and Sold

"Are not two sparrows sold for a farthing?" Everything in the universe—every object and every thought—is valued. Material things have a material value, spiritual things have a spiritual value, and to confound these values is not wise. To seek to purchase spiritual blessings with money, or material luxuries with virtue, is the way of selfishness and folly. It is to confound barter with religion and to make a religion of barter. Sympathy, kindness, love cannot be bought and sold; they can only be given and received. When a gift is paid for, it ceases to be a gift.

Because everything has a value, that which is freely given is gained with accumulation. He who gives up the lesser happiness of selfishness gains the greater happiness of unselfishness. The universe is just, and its justice is so perfect that he who has once perceived it can no more doubt or be afraid. He can only wonder and be glad.

Light on the Sense of Proportion

IN A NIGHTMARE there is no relation of one thing to another; all things are haphazard, and there is a general confusion and misery. Wise men have likened the self-seeking life to a nightmare. There is a close resemblance between a selfish life, in which the sense of proportion is so far lost that things are only seen as they affect one's own selfish aims, and in which there are feverish excitements and overwhelming troubles and disasters, and that state of troubled sleep known as nightmare.

In a nightmare, too, the controlling will and perceiving intelligence are asleep; and in a selfish life the better nature and spiritual perceptions are locked in profound slumber.

The uncultivated mind lacks the sense of

proportion. It does not see the right relation of one natural object to another, and is thereafter dead to the beauty and harmony with which it is surrounded.

And what is this sense of proportion but the faculty of seeing things as they are! It is a faculty which needs cultivating, and its cultivation, when applied to natural objects, embraces the entire intelligence and refines the moral character. It enters, however, into spiritual things as well as things natural, and here is more lacking, and more greatly needed. For to see things as they are in the spiritual sphere is to find no ground for grief, no lodging place for lamentation.

The Origin of All Suffering

Whence spring all this grief and anxiety, and fear and trouble? Is it not because things are not as men and women wish them to be? Is it not because the multiplicity of desires prevents them from seeing things in their true perspective and right proportion?

When one is overwhelmed with grief, he sees nothing but his loss; its nearness to him blots out the whole view of life. The thing in itself may be small, but to the sufferer it assumes a magnitude which is out of proportion to the surrounding objects of life.

All who have passed the age of thirty can look

back over their lives at times when they were perplexed with anxiety, overwhelmed with grief, or even, perhaps, on the verge of despair, over incidents which, seen now in their right proportion, are known to be very small.

If the would-be suicide will today stay his hand and wait, he will at the end of ten years marvel at his folly over so comparatively small a matter.

When the mind is possessed by passion or paralyzed with grief, it has lost the power of judgement. It cannot weigh and consider. It does not perceive the relative values and proportions of the things by which it is disturbed. Awake and acting, it yet moves in a nightmare which holds its faculties in thrall.

Prejudice is Blind

The passionate partisan lacks a sense of proportion to such an extent that, to him, his own side or view appears all that is right and good, and his opponent's all that is bad and wrong. To this partiality his reason is chained, so that whatever reason he may bring to bear upon the matter is enlisted in the service of bias, and is not exercised in order to find the just relation which exists between the two sides. He is so convinced that his own party is all right, and the other, equally intelligent party is all wrong, that it is impossible for him to be impartial and just. The only thing he understands as justice is that of getting his own way, or placing some ruling power in the hands of his party.

The Spiritual Sense of Proportion

Just as the sense of proportion in things material puts an end to the spirit of repugnance, so in things spiritual it puts an end to the spirit of strife. The true artist does not see ugliness anywhere; he sees only beauty. That which is loathsome to others fills, to him, its rightful place in nature, and it appears in his picture as a thing of beauty. The true seer does not see evil anywhere; he sees universal good. That which is hateful to others, he sees in its rightful place in the scheme of evolution, and it is held dispassionately in his mind as an object of contemplation.

Men and women worry, and grieve, and fight because they lack this sense of proportion, because they do not see things in their right relations. The objects of their turbulence are not things-in-themselves, but their own opinions about things, self-created shadows, the unreal creations of an egoistic nightmare.

The cultivation and development of the ethical sense of proportion converts the heated partisan into a gentle peacemaker, and gives the calm and searching of the prophet to the hitherto blind instrument in the clashing play of selfish forces.

The spiritual sense of proportion gives sanity; it restores the mind to calmness; it bestows impartiality and justice and reveals a universe of faultless harmony.

Light on Adherence to Principle

THE MAN OF TRUTH never departs from the divine principles which he has espoused. He may be threatened with sickness, poverty, pain, loss of friends and position, yea, even with immediate death, yet he does not desert the principles which he knows to be eternally true. To him, there is one thing more grievous, more to be feared and shunned than all the above evils put together, and that is—the desertion of principle. To turn coward in the hour of trial, to deny conscience, to join the rabble of passions, desires, and fears in turning upon, accusing, and crucifying the Eternal Christ of Divine Principle, because, forsooth, that principle has not given him personal health, affluence and ease—this, to the man of Truth, is the evil of evils, the sin of sins.

We cannot escape sickness and death. Though we avoid them for a long time, in the end they will overtake us. But we can avoid wrongdoing, we can avoid fear and cowardice. When we habitually avoid wrongdoing and cast out fear, the evils of life will not subdue us when they overtake us, for we shall have mastered them. Instead of avoiding them for a season we shall have conquered them on their own ground.

Standing Up to Your Highest Truth

There are those that teach that it is right to do wrong when the wrong is to protect another; that it is good, for instance, to tell a lie when its object is the well-being of another—that is, that it is right to desert a principle of truthfulness under severe trial. Such teaching has never emanated from the lips of the Great Teachers. It has not been uttered even by those lesser, yet superbly noble men, the prophets, saints and martyrs, for those divinely illuminated men knew full well that no circumstance can make a wrong a right, and that a lie has no saving and protective power. Wrongdoing is a greater evil than pain, and a lie is more deadly and destructive than death. Jesus rebuked Peter for trying to shield his Master's life by wrongdoing, and no right-minded person would accept life at the expense of the moral character of another when it appeared possible to do so.

All men admire and revere the martyrs, those steadfast men and women who feared wrong, cowardice, and lying, but who did not fear pain and death; those who were steadfast and calm in their adherence to principle even when brought to the utmost extremity of trial. Yea, even when the taunts and jeers of enemies assailed them, and the tears and agonies of loved ones appealed to them, they flinched not nor turned back, knowing that the future good and salvation of the whole world depended upon their firmness in that supreme hour. For this, they stand through all time as monuments of virtue, centers of saving, and uplifting power for all humankind.

But he who lied to save himself, or for the sake of the two or three beings whom he personally loved, is rarely heard of, for in the hour of desertion of principle, his power was gone. If he is heard of, he is not loved for that lie. He is always looked upon as one who fell when the test was applied; as an example of the highest virtue he is rejected by all men in all times.

Had all men believed that an untruth was right under extreme circumstances, we should have had no martyrs and saints, the moral fiber of humanity would have been undermined, and the world left to grope in ever deepening darkness.

Principles Are Our Salvation

The attitude which regards wrongdoing for the sake of others as the right thing to do is based on the tacit assumption that wrong and untruth are inferior evils to unhappiness, pain, and death. But the man of moral insight knows that wrong and untruth are the greater evils, and so he never commits them, even though his own life or the lives of others appear to be at stake.

It is easy for a man in the flowery time of ease or the heyday of prosperity to persuade himself that he is staunchly adhering to principle. But when pain overtakes him, when the darkness of misfortune begins to settle down upon him, and the pressure of circumstances hems him in—then he is on his trial, then he has come to the testing time. In that season it will be brought to light whether he clings to self or adheres to Truth.

Principles are for our salvation in the hour of need. If we desert them in that hour, how can we be saved from the snares and pains of self?

If a man does wrong to his conscience, thinking

thereby to avoid some immediate or pressing pain, he does not but increase pain and evil. The good man is less anxious to avoid pain than wrongdoing.

There is neither wisdom nor safety in deserting permanent and protective principles when our happiness seems to be at stake. If we desert the true for the pleasant, we shall lose both the pleasant and the true. But if we desert the pleasant for the true, the peace of truth will soothe away our sorrow.

If we barter the higher for the lower, emptiness and anguish will overtake us, and then, having abandoned the Eternal, where is our rock of refuge? But if we yield up the lower for the higher, the strength and satisfaction of the higher will remain with us, fullness of joy will overtake us, and we shall find in truth a rock of refuge from the evils and sorrows of life.

To find the permanent amid all the changes of life, and, having found it, adhere to it under all circumstances—this only is true happiness, this only is salvation and lasting peace.

Light on the Sacrifice of the Self

SELF-SACRIFICE IS ONE of the fundamental principles in the teachings of the Great Spiritual Masters. It consists in yielding up self, or selfishness, so that Truth may become the source of conduct. Self is not an entity that has to be cast out, but a condition of mind that has to be converted.

The renunciation of self is not the annihilation of the intelligent being, but the annihilation of every dark and selfish desire. Self is the blind clinging to perishable things and transient pleasures as distinguished from the intelligent practice of virtue and righteousness. Self is the lusting, coveting, desiring of the heart, and it is this that must be yielded up before Truth can be known, with its abiding calm and endless peace.

To give up things will not avail; it is the lust for things that must be sacrificed. Though a man sacrifice wealth, position, friends, family, fame, home, wife, child—yea, and life also—it will avail nothing if self is not renounced.

Buddha renounced the world and all that it held dear to him, but for six years he wandered and searched and suffered and not till he yielded up the desires of the heart did he become enlightened and arrive at peace.

By giving up only the objects of self-indulgence, no peace will ensue, but torment will follow. It is self-indulgence, the desire for the object, that must be abandoned—then peace enters the heart.

Sacrificing the Self

Sacrifice is painful so long as there is any vestige of self remaining in the heart. While there remains in the heart a lurking desire for an unworthy object or pleasure that has been sacrificed, there will be periods of intense suffering and fierce temptation. But when the desire for the unworthy object or pleasure is put away forever from the mind, and the sacrifice is complete and perfect, then, concerning that particular object or pleasure, there can be no more suffering or temptation. So when self in its entirety is sacrificed, sacrifice, in its painful aspect, is at an end, and perfect knowledge and perfect peace are reached.

Hatred is self. Covetousness is self. Envy and jealousy are self. Vanity and boasting are self. Gluttony and sensuality are self. Lying and deception are self. Speaking evil of one's neighbor is self. Anger and revenge are self.

Self-sacrifice consists in yielding up all these dark conditions of mind and heart. The process is a painful one in its early stages, but soon a divine peace descends at intervals upon the pilgrim. Later, this peace remains longer with him, and finally, when the rays of Truth begin to be radiated in the heart, remains with him.

This sacrifice leads to peace; for in the perfect life of Truth, there is no more sacrifice, and no more pain and sorrow. For where there is no more self there is nothing to be given up. Where there is no clinging of the mind to perishable things there is nothing to be renounced. Where all has been laid on the altar of Truth, selfish love is swallowed up in divine love. And in divine love there is no thought of self, for there is the perfection of insight, enlightenment, and immortality, and therefore perfect peace.

Light on the Management of the Mind

FOLLOWING THE LAST CHAPTER, a few hints on the management of one's mind will doubtless be opportune. Before a man can see even the necessity for thorough and complete self-government, he will have to throw off a great delusion in which so many are involved—the delusion of believing that his lapses of conduct are entirely due to those about him, and not entirely to himself.

"I could make far greater progress if I were not hindered by others," or "It is impossible for me to make any headway, seeing that I live with such irritable people," are commonly expressed complaints which spring from the error of imagining that others are responsible for one's own folly.

The violent or irritable man always blames those

about him for his fits of anger, and by continually living in this delusion, he becomes more and more confirmed in his rashness and perturbations. For how can a man overcome—nay, how can he even try to overcome, his weakness if he convinces himself that it springs entirely from the actions of others? Moreover, firmly believing this as he does, he vents his anger more and more upon others in order to try to make matters better for himself, and so becomes completely lost to all knowledge of the real origin of his unhappy state.

Men cast the blame of their unprosperous acts
Upon the abettors of their own resolve,
Or anything but their weak guilty selves.

Being Responsible for Every Action

All a man's weaknesses, sins, and falls take rise in his own heart, and he alone is responsible for them. It is true there are tempters and provokers, but temptations and provocations are powerless to him who refuses to respond to them. Tempters and provokers are but foolish men, and he who gives way to them has become a willing cooperator in their folly. He is unwise and weak, and the source of troubles is in himself. The pure man cannot be tempted; the wise man cannot be provoked.

Let a man fully realize that he is absolutely responsible for his every action, and he has already gone a considerable distance along the path which leads to wisdom and peace, for he will then commence to utilize temptation as a means of growth, and the wrong conduct of others he will regard as a test of his own strength.

The Virtue of Patience

Socrates thanked the gods for the gift of a shrewish wife in that it enabled him the better to cultivate the virtue of patience. It is a simple and easily perceived truth that we can better grow patient by living with the impatient, better grow unselfish by living with the selfish. If a man is impatient with the impatient, he is himself impatient. If he is selfish with the selfish, then he is himself selfish. The test and measure of virtue is trial, and, like gold and precious stones, the more it is tested the brighter it shines. If a man thinks he has virtue, yet gives way when its opposing vice is presented to him, let him not delude himself—he has not yet attained to the possession of that virtue.

Cease Blaming Others

If a man would rise and become a man indeed, let him cease to think the weak and foolish thought, "I am hindered by others," and let him set about to discover that he is hindered only by himself. Let him realize that the giving way to another is but a revelation of his own imperfection, and lo! upon him will descend the light of wisdom, and the door of peace will open unto him, and he will soon become the conqueror of self.

The fact that a man is continually troubled and disturbed by close contact with others is an indication that he requires such contact to impel him onward to a clearer comprehension of himself; and toward a higher and more steadfast state of mind.

The very things which he regards as insurmountable hindrances will become to him the most valuable aids when he fully realizes his moral responsibility and his innate power to do right. He will then cease to blame others for his unmanly conduct, and will commence to live steadfastly under all circumstances. The scales of self-delusion will quickly fall from his eyes, and he will then see that often when he imagined himself provoked, he himself was really the provoker. As he rises above his own mental disturbances the necessity for coming in contact with the same condition in others will cease, and he will pass, by a natural process, into the company of the good and the pure. He will then awaken in others the nobility which he has arrived at in himself.

Be noble! and the nobleness that lies
In other men, sleeping, but never dead,
Will rise in majesty to meet thine own.

Light on Self-Control: The Door of Heaven

THE FOREMOST LESSON which the world has to learn on its way to wisdom is the lesson of self-control. All the bitter punishments which men undergo in the school of experience are inflicted because they have failed to learn this lesson. Apart from self-control, salvation is a meaningless word, and peace is an impossibility. For how can a man be saved from any sin while he continues to give way to it? Or how can he realize abiding peace until he has conquered and subdued the troubles and disturbances of his mind?

Self-control is the Door of Heaven; it leads to light and peace. Without it a man is already in hell; he is lost in darkness and unrest. Men inflict upon themselves far-reaching sufferings, and pass through indescribable torments, both of body and soul, through lack of self-control. Not until they resort to its practice can their sufferings and torments pass away. For it has no substitute, nothing can take its place, and there is no power in the universe that can do for a man that which he, sooner or later, must do for himself by entering the practice of self-control.

Self-Control Manifests as Divine Power

By self-control a man manifests his divine power and ascends toward divine wisdom and perfection. Every man can practice it. The weakest man can begin now, and until he does begin, his weakness will remain, or he will become weaker still.

Calling or not calling upon God or Jesus, Brahma or Buddha, Spirits or Masters, will not avail men who refuse to govern themselves and purify their hearts. Believing or disbelieving that Jesus is God, that Buddha is omniscient, or the Spirits or Masters guide human affairs, cannot help men who continue to cling to the elements of strife and ignorance and corruption within themselves.

What theological affirmation or denial can justify, or what outward power put right, the man who refuses to abandon a slanderous or abusive tongue, or give up an angry temper, or to sacrifice his impure imaginings? The flower reaches the upper light by first contending with the under darkness, and man can only reach the Light of Truth by striving against the darkness within himself.

The Gate of Heaven

The vast importance of self-control is not realized by men, its absolute necessity is not apprehended by them, and the spiritual freedom and glory to which it leads are hidden from their eyes. Because of this, men are enslaved and misery and suffering ensue. Let a man contemplate the violence, impurity, disease, and suffering which occur upon earth, and consider how much of it is due to want of self-control, and he will gradually come to realize the great need there is for self-control.

I say again that self-control is the Gate of Heaven, for without it neither happiness nor love nor peace can be realized and maintained. In the degree that it is lacked by a man, in just that measure will his mind and life be given over to confusion. And it is because such a large number of individuals have not yet learned to practice it that the enforced restraint of national laws is required for the maintenance of law and order and the prevention of destructive confusion.

Religion is Purity of Mind

Self-control is the beginning of virtue, and it

leads to the acquisition of every noble attribute. It is the first essential quality in a well-ordered and truly religious life, and it leads to calmness, blessedness and peace. Without it, although there may be theological belief or profession, there can be no true religion, for what is religion but enlightened conduct? And what is spirituality but the triumph over the unruly tendencies of the mind?

When men both depart from and refuse to practice self-control, they fall into the great and dark delusion of separating religion from conduct. Then they persuade themselves that religion consists not in overcoming self and living blamelessly, but in holding a certain belief about Scripture, and in worshiping a certain Savior in a particular way. Hence arise the innumerable complications and confusions of letter-worship, and the violence and bitter strife into which men fall in defense of their own formulated religion.

But true religion cannot be formulated; it is purity of mind, a loving heart, a soul at peace with the world. It need not be defended, for it is Being and Doing and Living. A man begins to practice religion when he begins to control himself.

Light on Acts and Their Consequences

ONE OF THE COMMONEST EXCUSES for wrongdoing is that, if right were done, calamity would ensue. Thus the foolish concern themselves, not with the act, but with the consequence of the act, a foreknowledge of which is assumed. The desire to secure pleasant results, and to escape unpleasant consequences, is at the root of that confusion of mind which renders men incapable of distinguishing between good and evil, and prevents them from practicing the one and abandoning the other. Even when it is claimed that the wrong thing is done, not for one's self, but in order to secure the happiness of others, the delusion is the same, only it is more subtle and dangerous.

The wise concern themselves with the act, and not

with its consequences. They consider, not what is pleasant or unpleasant, but what is right. Thus doing what is right only, and not straining after results, they are relieved of all burdens of doubt, desire, and fear. Nor can one who so acts ever become so involved in an extricable difficulty, or be troubled with painful perplexity. His course is so simple, straight, and plain that he can never be confused with misgivings and uncertainties.

Those who so act are said by Krishna to act "without regard to the fruits of action," and he further declares that those who have thus renounced results are supremely good, supremely wise.

Cease Working for Results

Those who work for pleasant results only, and who depart from the right path when their own, or others' happiness appears to be at stake, cannot escape doubt, difficulty, perplexity, and pain. Ever forecasting probable consequences, they act in one way today, and in another way tomorrow. Unstable and blown about by the changing wind of circumstance, they become more and more bewildered, and the consequences about which they trouble do not accrue.

But they who work for righteousness only, who

are careful to do the right act, putting away all selfish considerations, all thought of results, they are steadfast, unchanging, untroubled, and at peace amid all vicissitudes, and the fruits of their acts are ever sweet and blessed.

Even the knowledge, which only the righteous possess, that wrong acts can never produce good results, and that right acts can never bring about bad results, is in itself fraught with sweet assurance and peace. For whether the fruits of acts are sought or unsought, they cannot be escaped.

They who sow to self, and, ignorant of the law of Truth, think they can make their own results, reap the bitter fruits of self.

They who sow to righteousness, knowing themselves to be the reapers, and not the makers of the consequences, reap the sweet fruits of righteousness.

Right is supremely simple, and is without complexity. Error is interminably complex, and involves the mind in confusion.

To put away self and passion, and establish one's self in right-doing, this is the highest wisdom.

Light on the Way of Wisdom

THE PATH OF WISDOM is the highest way, the way in which all doubt and uncertainty are dispelled and knowledge and surety are realized.

Amid the excitements and pleasures of the world and the surging whirlpools of human passions, Wisdom—so calm, so silent and so beautiful—is indeed difficult to find, difficult, not because of its incomprehensible complexity, but because of its unobtrusive simplicity, and because self is so blind and rash, and so jealous of its rights and pleasures.

Wisdom Is the Enemy of Self

Wisdom is "rejected of men" because it always comes right home to one's self in the form of wounding reproof, and the lower nature of man cannot bear to be reproved. Before Wisdom can be acquired, self must be wounded to the death, and because of this, because Wisdom is the enemy of self, self rises in rebellion, and will not be overcome and denied.

The foolish man is governed by his passions and personal cravings. When about to do anything he does not ask "Is this right?" but only considers how much pleasure or personal advantage he will gain by it. He does not govern his passions and act from fixed principles, but is the slave of his inclinations and follows where they lead.

The wise man governs his passions and puts away all personal cravings. He never acts from impulse and passion, but dispassionately considers what is right to be done, and does it. He is always thoughtful and self-possessed, and guides his conduct by the loftiest moral principles. He is superior to both pleasure and pain.

Wisdom Is Right Action

Wisdom cannot be found in books or travel, in learning or philosophy; it is acquired by practice only. A man may read the precepts of the greatest sages continually, but if he does not purify and govern himself he will remain foolish. A man may be intimately conversant with the writings of the greatest philosophers, but so long as he continues to give way to his passions he will not attain to wisdom.

Wisdom is right action, right doing; folly is wrong action, wrong doing. All reading, all studying is vain if man will not see his errors and give them up.

Wisdom says to the vain man, "Do not praise yourself," to the proud man, "Humble yourself," to the gossip, "Govern your tongue," to the angry man, "Subdue your anger," to the resentful man, "Forgive your enemy," to the self-indulgent man, "Be temperate," to the impure man, "Purge your heart of lust," and to all men, "Beware of small faults, do your duty faithfully, and never intermeddle with the duty of another."

Annihilating the Self

These things are very simple; the doing of them is simple. But as it leads to the annihilation of self, the selfish tendencies in a man object to them and rise up in revolt against them, loving their own life of turbulent excitement and feverish pleasure, and hating the calm and beautiful silence of Wisdom. Thus men remain in folly.

Nevertheless, the Way of Wisdom is always open, is always ready to receive the tread of the pilgrim who has grown weary of the thorny and intricate ways of folly. No man is prevented from becoming wise but by himself. No man can acquire Wisdom but by his own exertions. And he who is prepared to be honest with himself, to measure the depths of his ignorance, to come face to face with his errors, to recognize and acknowledge his faults, and at once to set about the task of his own regeneration, such a man will find the way of Wisdom. Walking with humble and obedient feet, he will, in due time, come to the sweet City of Deliverance.

Light on Disposition

I CANNOT HELP IT, it is my disposition." How often one hears this expression as an excuse for wrongdoing. What does it imply? This, that the person who utters it believes that he has no choice in the matter, that he cannot alter his character. He believes that he must go on doing the wrong thing to the end of his days because he was "born so," or because his father or grandfather was like that; or, if not these, then someone along the family line a hundred, or two or three hundred years ago must have been afflicted, and therefore he is and must remain so. Such a belief should be uprooted, destroyed, and cast away, for it is not only without reason, it is a complete barrier to all progress, to all growth in goodness, to all development of character and noble expansion of life.

Character is not permanent; it is, indeed, one of the most changeable things in nature. If not changed by a conscious act of the will, it is being continually modified and reformed by the pressure of circumstances. Disposition is not fixed, except insofar as one fixes it by continuing to do the same thing, and by persistence in the stubborn belief that he "cannot help it." As soon as one gets rid of that belief he will find that he can help it. Further, he will find that intelligence and will are instruments which can mold disposition to any extent, and that, too, with considerable rapidity if one is in earnest.

What is disposition but a habit formed by repeating the same thing over and over again? Cease repeating (doing) the thing, and lo! the disposition is changed, the character is altered. To cease from an old habit of thought or action is, I know, difficult at first, but with each added effort the difficulty decreases, and finally disappears, and then the new and good habit is formed and the disposition is changed from bad to good, the character is ennobled, the mind is delivered from torment and is lifted into joy.

There is no need for anyone to remain the slave of a disposition which causes him unhappiness, and which he himself regards as undesirable. He can abandon it. He can break away from the slavery. He can deliver himself and be free.

Light on Individual Liberty

WITHIN THE SPHERE of his own mind man has all power, but in the sphere of other minds and outside things, his power is limited. He can command his own mind, but he cannot command the minds of others. He can choose what he shall think, but he cannot choose what others shall think. He cannot control the weather as he wills, but he can control his mind, and decide what his mental attitude toward the weather shall be.

A man can reform the dominion of his own mind, but he cannot reform the outer world because the outer world is composed of other minds having the same freedom of choice as himself. A pure being cannot cleanse the heart of one less pure, but by his life of purity and by elucidating his experience in the attainment of purity, he can, as a teacher, act as a guide to others, and so enable them more readily and rapidly to purify themselves. But even then those others have the power to decide whether they shall accept or reject such guidance, so complete is man's choice.

It is because of this dual truth—that man has no power in the realm of others' minds and yet has all power over his own mind, that he cannot avoid the consequences of his own thoughts and acts. Man is altogether powerless to alter or avert consequences, but he is altogether powerful in his choice of causative thought. Having chosen his thoughts, he must accept their full consequences. Having acted, he cannot escape the full results of his act.

Acknowledging Freedom of Thought

Law reigns universally, and there is perfect individual liberty. A man can do as he likes, but all other men can also do as they like. A man has power to steal, but others have the power to protect themselves against the thief. Having sent out his thought, having acted his purpose, a man's power over that thought and purpose is at an end. The consequences are certain and cannot be escaped, and they will be of the nature of the thought and act which produced them—painful or blessed.

Seeing that a man can think and do as he chooses, and that all others have the like liberty, a man has to learn, sooner or later, to reckon with other minds, and until he does this he will be ceaselessly involved in suffering. To think and act apart from the consideration of others is both an abuse and an infringement of liberty. Such thoughts and acts are annulled and brought to naught by the harmonizing Principle of Liberty itself, and such annulling and bringing to naught is felt by the individual as suffering.

When the mind, rising above ignorance, recognizes the magnitude of its power within its own sphere and ceases to antagonize itself against others, it harmonizes itself to those other minds. Having acknowledged their freedom of choice, it has then realized spiritual plenitude and the cessation of suffering.

The Ego Manifests Selfishness

Selfishness, egotism, and despotism are, from the spiritual standpoint, transferable terms; they are one and the same thing. Every selfish thought or act is a manifestation of egotism, is an effort of despotism, and it is met with suffering and defeat. It is annulled because the Law of Liberty cannot, in the smallest particular, be annulled.

If selfishness could conquer, Liberty would be nonexistent, but selfishness fails of all results but pain, because Liberty is supreme. An act of selfishness contains two elements of egotism: namely (1) the denial of liberty of others and (2) the assertion of one's own liberty beyond its legitimate sphere. It thereby destroys itself. Despotism is death.

Man is not the creature of selfishness, he is the maker of it. It is an indication of his power—his power to disobey even the law of his being. Selfishness is power without wisdom; it is energy wrongly directed. A man is selfish because he is ignorant of his nature and power as a mental being. Such ignorance and selfishness entail suffering, and by repeated suffering and age-long experience he at last arrives at knowledge and the legitimate exercise of his power. The truly enlightened man cannot be selfish: he cannot accuse others of selfishness, or try to coerce them into being unselfish.

Selfishness Brings Suffering

The selfish man is eager to bend others to his own way and will, believing it to be the only right way for all. He thereby ignorantly wastes himself in trying to check in others the power which he freely exercises himself, namely—the power to choose their own way and exercise their own will. By so doing, he places himself in direct antagonism with the like tendencies and freedom of other minds, and brings into operation the instruments of his own suffering. Hence, the ceaseless interplay of conflicting forces; the unending fires of passion; the turmoil, strife, and woe. Selfishness is misapplied power.

The unselfish man is he who, ceasing from all personal interference, abandons the "I" as the source of judgment. Having recognized his unlimited freedom through the abandonment of all egotism even in thought, he refrains from encroachment upon the boundless freedom of others. He realizes the legitimacy of their choice and their right to the free employment of their power.

However others may choose to act toward such a man, it can never cause him any trouble or suffering, because he is perfectly willing that they should so choose to act, and he harbors no wish that they should act in any other way. He realizes that his sole duty, as well as his entire power, lies in acting rightly toward them, and that he is in no way concerned with their actions toward him that is both their choice and their business. To the unselfish man, therefore, malice, envy, backbiting, jealousy, accusation, condemnation, and persecution have passed away. Having ceased to practice these things, he is not disturbed when they are hurled at him. Thus liberation from sin is liberation from suffering. The selfless man is free; he has made the servitude of sin impossible; he has broken every bond.

Light on the Blessing and Dignity of Work

THAT "LABOR IS LIFE" is a principle pregnant with truth, and one which cannot be too often repeated or too closely studied and practiced. Labor is so often regarded as an irksome and even degrading means of obtaining ease and pleasure, and not as what it really is—a thing happy and noble in itself. The lesson contained in the maxim needs to be taken to heart and more and more thoroughly learned.

Activity, both mental and physical, is the essence of life. The complete cessation of life is death, and death is immediately followed by corruption. Ease and death are closely related. The more there is of activity, the more abounding is life. The brain-worker, the original thinker, the man of unceasing mental activity, is the longest-lived man in a community. The agricultural laborer, the gardener, the man of unceasing physical activity comes next with length in years.

Don't Be Afraid of Work

Pure-hearted, healthy-minded people love work, and are happy in their labors. They never complain of being "overworked." It is very difficult, almost impossible, for a man to be overworked if he lives a sound and pure life. It is worry, bad habits, discontent and idleness that kill—especially idleness, for if labor is life, then idleness must be death. Let us get rid of sin before we talk about being overworked.

There are those who are afraid of work, regarding it as an enemy, and who fear a breakdown by doing too much. They have to learn what a health-bestowing friend work is. Others are ashamed of work, looking upon it as a degrading thing to be avoided. The "pure in heart and sound in head" are neither afraid nor ashamed of work, and they dignify whatsoever they undertake. No necessary work can be degrading, but if a man regards his work as such, he is already degraded, not by his task, but by his slavish vanity.

Man hath his daily work of body and mind
Appointed, which declares his dignity.

The idle man who is afraid of work, and the vain man who is ashamed of it, are both on the way to poverty, if they are not already there. The industrious man, who loves work, and the man of true dignity, who glorifies work, are both on their way to affluence, if they are not already there. The lazy man is sowing the seeds of poverty and crime; the vain man is sowing the seeds of humiliation and shame. The industrious man is sowing the seeds of affluence and virtue; the dignified worker is sowing the seeds of victory and honor. Deeds are seeds, and the harvest will appear in due season.

Rejoice in Your Work

There is a common desire to acquire riches with as little effort as possible, which is a kind of theft. To try to obtain the fruits of labor without laboring is to take the fruits of another man's labor; to try to get money without giving its equivalent is to take that which belongs to another and not one's self. What is theft but this frame of mind carried to its logical extreme?

Let us rejoice in our work. Let us rejoice that we have the strength and capacity for work, and let us increase that strength and capacity by unremitting labor.

Whatever our work may be, it is noble, and will be

perceived by the world as noble, if we perform it with a noble spirit. The virtuous do not despise any labor which falls on their lot. And he who works and faints not, who is faithful, patient, and uncompromising even in the time of poverty, he will surely at last eat of the sweet fruits of his labor. Yea, even while he labors and seems to fail, happiness will be his constant companion, for, "Blessed is the man that has found his work; let him ask no other blessedness."

Light on Good Manners and Refinement

Move upward, working out the beast,
And let the ape and tiger die.

ALL CULTURE IS GETTING AWAY from the beast. Evolution is a refining process, and the unwritten laws of society are inherent in the evolutionary law.

Education is intellectual culture. The scholar is engaged in purifying and perfecting his intellect; the spiritual devotee is engaged in purifying and perfecting his heart.

When a man aspires to nobler heights of achievement, and sets about the realization of his ideal, he commences to refine his nature; and the more pure a man makes himself within, the more refined, gracious, and gentle will be his outward demeanor.

Good manners have an ethical basis, and cannot

be divorced from religion. To be ill-mannered is to be imperfect, for what are ill manners but the outward expression of inward defects? What a man does, that he is. If he acts rudely, he is a rude man; if he acts foolishly, he is a foolish man; if he acts gently, he is a gentleman. It is a mistake to suppose that a man can have a gentle and refined mind behind a rough and brutal exterior (though such a man may possess some strong animal virtues), as the outer is an expression of the inner.

Right Conduct

One of the steps in the noble Eightfold Path to perfection as expounded by Buddha is—Right Conduct or Good Behavior. It should be plain to all that the man who has not yet learned how to conduct himself toward others in a kindly, gracious, and unselfish spirit has not yet entered the pathway of the holy life.

If a man refines his heart, he will refine his behavior; if he refines his behavior, it will help him to refine his heart.

To be coarse, brutish, and snappish may be natural to the beast, but the man who aspires to be even an endurable member of society (not to mention the higher manhood), will at once purge away any such bestial traits that may possess him.

All these things which aid in man's refinement—such as music, painting, poetry, manners—are servants and messengers of progress. Man degrades himself when he imitates the brute. Let us not mistake barbarism for simplicity or vulgarity for honesty.

Unselfishness, kindliness, and consideration for others will always be manifested outwardly as gentleness, graciousness, and refinement. To affect these graces by simulating them may seem to succeed, but it does not. Affectation and hypocrisy are soon divulged; every man's eye, sooner or later, pierces through their flimsiness, and ultimately none but the actors of them are deceived.

As Emerson says:

"What is done for effect, is seen to be done for effect; and what is done for love, is felt to be done for love."

Good Manners

Children who are well-bred are taught always to consider the happiness of others before their own: to offer others the most comfortable seat, the choicest fruit, the best tidbit, and so on, and also to do everything, even the most trivial acts, in the right way. And these two things—unselfishness and right action—are at the basis, not only of good manners, but of all ethics, religion, and true living: they represent power and skill. The selfish man is weak and unskillful in his actions. Unselfishness is the right way of thinking; good manners are the right way of acting.

As Emerson, again, says:

"There is always a way of doing everything, if it be to boil an egg. Manners are the happy way of doing things right."

A Right Way and a Wrong Way

It is a frequent error among men to imagine that the Higher Life is an ideal something quite above and apart from the common details of life, and that to neglect these or to perform them in a slovenly manner is an indication that the mind is preoccupied on "higher things." Whereas it is an indication that the mind is becoming inexact, dreamy, and weak, instead of exact, wide awake, and strong. No matter how apparently trivial the thing is which has to be done, there is a right way of doing it, and to do it in the right way saves friction, time, and trouble, conserves power, and develops grace, skill, and happiness.

The artisan has a variety of tools with which to ply his particular craft, and he is taught (and also finds by experience) that each tool must be applied to its special use, and never under any circumstances must one tool be made to do service for another. By using every tool in its proper place and in the right way, the maximum of dexterity and power is attained. Should a boy learning a trade refuse instruction, and persist in using the tools in his own way, making one tool do service for another, he would never become anything better than a clumsy bungler, and would be a failure in his trade.

It is the same throughout the whole life. If a man opens himself to receive instruction, and studies how to do everything rightly and lawfully, he becomes strong, skillful, and wise, master of himself, his thoughts and actions. But if he persists in following his momentary impulses, in doing everything as he feels prompted, not exercising thoughtfulness, and rejecting instruction, such a man will attain to nothing better than a slovenly and bungling life.

The Universe Demands Right Doing

Confucius paid the strictest attention to dress,

eating, deportment, passing speech—to all the so-called trivialities of life, as well as to the momentous affairs of state and the lofty moral principles which he expounded. He taught his disciples that it is the sign of a vulgar and foolish mind to regard anything as "trivial" that is necessary to be done, that the wise man pays attention to all his duties, and does everything wisely, thoughtfully, and rightly.

It is not an arbitrary edict of society that the man who persists in eating with his knife be rejected, for a knife is given to cut with, and a fork to eat with, and to put things to wrong and slovenly uses—even in the passing details of life—does not make for progress, but is retrogressive and makes for confusion.

It is not a despotic condition in the law of things that so long as a man persists in thinking and acting unkindly toward others he shall be shut out from Heaven. He shall remain in the outer pain and unrest, for selfishness is disruption and disorder. The universe is sustained by exactness, it rests on order, it demands right doing, and the searcher of wisdom will watch all his ways. He will think purely, speak gently, and act graciously, refining his entire nature, both in the letter and the spirit.

Light on Diversities of Creeds

THOSE WHO DEPART from the common track in matters of faith, and strike out independently in search of the Higher Life, as distinguished from the letter of religious dogma, are apt to sink into a pitfall which awaits them at the first step, namely, the pitfall of pride.

Attacking "creeds" and speaking contemptuously of "the orthodox" (as though orthodoxy were synonymous with evil) are not uncommon practices among those who fondly imagine they are in possession of greater spiritual light. Departure from orthodoxy does not by any means include departure from sin. Indeed, it is frequently accompanied with increased bitterness and contempt. Change of opinion is one thing, change of heart is quite another. To withdraw one's adherence from creeds is easy; to withdraw one's self from sin is more difficult.

Hatred and pride, and not necessarily orthodoxy and conformity, are the things to be avoided. One's own sin, and not another man's creed, is the thing to be despised.

The right-minded man cannot pride himself on being "broader" than others, or assume that he is on a "higher plane" than others, or think with self-righteous contempt of those who still cling to some form of letter worship which he has abandoned.

Applying the words "narrow," "bigoted," and "selfish" to others, is not the indication of an enlightened mind. No person would wish these terms to be applied to himself, and he who is becoming truly religious does not speak of others in words which would wound him were they directed toward himself.

Love Brings Together All Creeds

Those who are learning how to exercise humility and compassion are becoming truly enlightened. Thinking lowly of themselves and kindly of others; condemning their own sins with merciless logic, and thinking with tender pity of the sins of others, they develop that insight into the nature and law of things which enables them to see the truth that is in others, and in the religions of others. They do not condemn their neighbor because he holds a different faith, or because he adheres to a formal creed. Creeds must be, and he who performs faithfully his duty in his own particular creed, not interfering with or condemning his neighbor in the performance of his duty, is bringing the world nearer to perfection and peace.

Amid all the diversities of creeds there is a unifying power of undying and unalterable Love—and he or she who has Love has entered into sympathetic union with all.

He who has acquired the true spirit of Religion, who has attained to pure insight and deep charity of heart, will avoid all strife and condemnation. He will not fall into the delusion of praising his own sect (should he belong to one) and try to prove that it alone is right, or disparage other sects and try to prove that they are false. As the true man does not speak in praise of himself or his own work, so the man of humility, charity, and wisdom does not speak of his own sect as being superior to all others. He does not seek to elevate his own particular religion by picking holes in forms of faith which are held sacred by others.

The Edict of Asoka

Nothing more explicit and magnanimous has ever been uttered, in reference to this particular phrase of the practice of charity, than is found in the twelfth Edict of Asoka, the great Indian Ruler and Saint who lived some two or three centuries previous to the Christian era, and whose life, dedicated to the spread of Truth, testified to the beauty of his words. The edict runs thus:

"There should be no praising of one's own sect and decrying of other sects; but, on the contrary, a rendering of honor to other sects for whatever cause honor may be due. By so doing, both one's own sect may be helped forward, and other sects will be benefited; by acting otherwise, one's own sect will be destroyed in injuring others. Whosoever exalts his own sect by decrying others does so doubtless out of love for his own sect, thinking to spread abroad the fame thereof. But, on the contrary, he inflicts the more an injury upon his own sect."

These are wise and holy words; the breath of charity is in them, and they may be well pondered upon by those who are anxious to overthrow, not the religions of other men, but their own shortcomings.

It is a dark and deep-seated delusion that causes a man to think he can best advance the cause of his religion by exposing what he regards as the "evils" of other religions. The most part of it is, that while such a one rejoices in the thought that by continually belittling other sects he will perhaps at last wipe them out, and win all men to his side, he is all the time engaged in the sad work of bringing into disrepute, and thereby destroying, his own sect.

Just as every time a man slanders another, he inflicts lasting injury upon his own character and prospects, so every time one speaks evil of another sect, he soils and demeans his own. And the man who is prone to attack and condemn other religions is the one who suffers most when his own religion is attacked and condemned.

If a man does not like that his own religion should be denounced as evil and false, he should carefully guard himself that he does not condemn other religions as such. If it pleases him when his own cause is well spoken of and helped, he should speak well of and help other causes which, while differing from his own in method, have the same good view in end. In this way he will escape the errors and miseries of sectarian strife, and will perfect himself in divine charity.

Avoid Divisions and Distinctions

The heart that has embraced gentleness and charity avoids all those blind passions which keep the fires of party strife, violence, persecution, and bitterness burning from age to age. It dwells in thoughts of pity and tenderness, scorning nothing, despising nothing, and not stirring up animosity. For he who acquires gentleness gains that clear insight into the Great Law which cannot be obtained in any other way. He sees that there is good in all sects and religions, and he makes that good his own.

Let the truth-seeker avoid divisions and offending distinctions, and let him strive after charity; for charity does not slander, backbite, or condemn. It does not think of trampling down another's, and elevating its own.

Contradiction Springs from Error

Truth cannot contradict itself. The nature of Truth is exactness, reality, undeviating certitude. Why, then, the ceaseless conflict between the religions and creeds? Is it not because of error? Contradiction and conflict belong to the domain of error, for error, being confusion, is in the nature of self-contradiction. If the Christian says, "My religion is true and Buddhism is false," and if the Buddhist says, "Christianity is false and Buddhism is true," we are confronted with an irreconcilable contradiction, for these two religions cannot be both true and false. Such a contradiction cannot come from Truth, and must therefore spring from error.

But if both these religious partisans should now say or think, "Yes, truly the contradiction springs from error, but the error is in the other man and his religion, and not me and mine," this does but intensify the contradiction. From where, then, springs the error, and where is Truth? Does not the very attitude of mind which these men adopt toward each other constitute the error? And were they to reverse that attitude, exchanging antagonism for good will, would they not perceive the Truth which does not stand in conflict with itself?

The man who says, "My religion is true, and my neighbor's is false," has not yet discovered the truth in his own religion, for when a man has done that, he will see the Truth in all religions. As behind all the universal phenomena there is but one Truth, so behind all the religions and creeds there is but one religion. For every religion contains the same ethical teaching, and all the Great Teachers taught exactly the same thing.

Truth is a Pure Heart

The precepts of the Sermon on the Mount are to be found in all religions. The life which these precepts demand was lived by all the Great Teachers and many of their disciples, for the Truth is a pure heart and a blameless life, and not a set of dogmas and opinions. All religions teach purity of heart, holiness of life, compassion, love, and good will. They teach the doing of good deeds and the giving up of selfishness and sin. These things are not dogmas, theologies, and opinions; they are things to be done, to be practiced, to be lived. Men do not differ about these things, for they are the acknowledged verities of every sect. What, then, do they differ about? About their opinions, their speculations, their theologies.

Men differ about that which is unreal, not that which is real; they fight over error, and not over Truth. The very essential of all religion (and religions) is that before a man can know anything of Truth, he must cease from fighting his fellow man, and shall learn to regard him with good will and love. How can a man do this while he is convinced that his neighbor's religion is false, and that it is his duty to do all that he can to undermine and overthrow it? This is not doing unto others as we would that they should do to us.

All Religions the Same

That which is true and real is true and real everywhere and always. There is no distinction between the pious Christian and the pious Buddhist. Purity of heart, piety of life, holy aspirations, and the love of Truth are the same in the Buddhist as the Christian. The good deeds of the Buddhist are not different from the good deeds of the Christian. Remorse for sin and sorrow for wrong thoughts and deeds springs in the hearts, not only of Christians, but of men and women of all religions. Great is the need of sympathy. Great is the need of love.

All religions are the same in that they teach the same fundamental truths. But men, instead of practicing these truths, engage in opinions and speculations about things which are outside the range of knowledge and experience, and it is in defending and promulgating their own particular speculations that men become divided and engage in conflict with each other.

Condemnation is the beginning of persecution. The thought, "I am right and you are wrong," is a seed prolific of hatred. It was out of this seed that the Spanish Inquisition grew. He who would find the universal Truth must abandon egotism and quench the hateful flames of condemnation. He must remove from his heart the baneful thought, "All others are wrong," and think the illuminating thought, "It is I who am wrong." And having thus thought, he will cease from sin, and will live in love and good will toward all, making no distinctions, engaging in no divisions, a peacemaker and not a partisan. Thus living charitably disposed to all, he will become one with all. He will comprehend the Universal Truth, the Eternal Religion; for while error and selfishness divide, Truth demonstrates Truth and Religion unifies.

Light on Law and Miracle

THE LOVE OF THE WONDERFUL is an element in human nature which, like passions and desires, requires to be curbed, directed, and finally transmuted; otherwise superstition and the obscuration of reason and insight cannot be avoided. The idea of a miracle must be transcended before the orderly, eternal, and beneficent nature of the law can be perceived. Then peace and certainty, which a knowledge of law bestows, can be enjoyed.

Just as a child when its eyes are opened to the phenomena of this world becomes involved in wonder, and revels in tales of giants and fairies, so when a man first opens his mental eyes to spiritual things does he become involved in stories of marvels and miracles. As a child at last becomes a man and leaves behind the crudities of childhood, understanding more accurately the relative nature of the phenomena around him, so with a fuller spiritual development and greater familiarity with the inner realities a man at last leaves behind the era of childish wonderment. He comes into touch with the law of things, and governs his life by principles that are fixed and invariable.

The Law is Orderly

Law is universal and eternal, and, although vast areas of knowledge are waiting to be revealed, cause and effect will ever prevail. Every new discovery, every truth revealed, will serve to bring one nearer to a realization of the beauty, stability, and supremacy of the law. And very gladdening it is to know that law is inviolable and eternal throughout every department of nature. For then we know that the same operations of the universe are ever the same, and can therefore be discovered, understood, obeyed. This is a ground of certainty, and therefore of great hope and joy. The idea of miracle is a denial of law and the substitution of an arbitrary and capricious power.

Do Not Desire Miracles

It is true that around the lives of the Great Teachers of humanity stories of miracles have grown, but they have emanated from the undeveloped minds of the people, not from the Teachers themselves.

Lao-Tze expounded the Supreme Law, or Reason, which admits no miracle, yet his religion has today become so corrupted with the introduction of the marvelous as to be little better than a mass of superstition.

Even Buddhism, whose founder declared that, "Seeing that the Law of Karma (cause and effect) governs all things, the disciple who aims at performing miracles does not understand the doctrine," and that, "The desire to perform miracles arises either from covetousness or vanity," has surrounded, in its corrupted form, the life of its Great Master with a number of miracles.

Even during the lifetime of Ramakrishna, the Hindu teacher who died in 1886, and who is regarded by his disciples as an incarnation of Deity to this age, all sorts of miracles were attributed to him by the people, and are now associated with his name. Yet, according to Max Muller, these miracles are without any foundation of evidence or fact, and Ramakrishna himself ridiculed and repudiated miracle.

Understand the Law Is Orderly

As men become more enlightened, miracles and

wonder-working will be expunged from religion, and the orderly beauty of Law and the ethical grandeur of obedience to the Law will become revealed and known. No man who desires to perform miracles or astral or psychological wonders, who is curious to see invisible or supernatural beings, or who is ambitious to become a "Master" or an "Adept," can attain a clear perception of Truth and the living of the highest life.

Childish wonderment about things must be supplanted by knowledge of things, and vanity is a complete barrier to the entrance of the true path which demands of the disciple lowliness of heart, humility. He is on the true path who is cultivating kindness, forbearance, and a loving heart. The marks of a true Master are not miracles and wonder-working, but infinite patience, boundless compassion, spotless purity, and a heart at peace with all.

Light on War and Peace

WAR SPRINGS FROM INWARD STRIFE. "War in heaven" precedes war on earth. When the inward spiritual harmony is destroyed by division and conflict, it will manifest itself outwardly in the form of war. Without this inward conflict war could not be, nor can war cease until the inward harmony is restored.

War consists of aggression and resistance, and after the fight has commenced both combatants are like aggressors and resisters. Thus the effort to put an end to war by aggressive means produces war.

"I have set myself stubbornly against the war spirit," said a man a short time ago. He did not know that he was, by that attitude of mind, practicing and fostering the war spirit.

To fight against war is to produce war. It is impossible to fight for peace, because all fighting is the annihilation of peace. To think of putting an end to war by denouncing and fighting it is the same as if one should try to quench fire by throwing straw upon it.

The Spirit of Peace

He, therefore, who is truly a person of peace, does not resist war, but practices peace. He, therefore, who takes sides and practices attack and defense is responsible for war, for he is always at war in his mind. He cannot know the nature of peace, for he has not arrived at peace in his own heart.

The true man of peace is he who has put away from his mind the spirit of quarreling and party strife, who neither attacks others nor defends himself, and whose heart is at peace with all. Such a man has already laid in his heart the foundations of the empire of peace; he is a peacemaker, for he is at peace with the whole world and practices the spirit of peace under all circumstances.

Very beautiful is the spirit of peace, and it says, "Come and rest." Bickerings, quarreling, party divisions—these must be forever abandoned by him who would establish peace.

War will continue so long as men will allow themselves, individually, to be dominated by passion, and only when men have quelled the inward tumult will the outward horror pass away.

Self is the great enemy, the producer of all strife, and the maker of many sorrows. He, therefore, who will bring about peace on earth, let him overcome egotism, let him subdue his passions, let him conquer himself.

Light on the Brotherhood of Man

THERE IS NO LACK OF WRITING and preaching about "universal brotherhood," and it has been adopted as a leading article of faith by many newly formed societies. But what is so urgently needed to begin with is not universal brotherhood, but particular Brotherhood. That is, the adoption of a magnanimous, charitable, and kindly spirit toward those with whom we come in immediate contact; toward those who contradict, oppose and attack us, as well as toward those who love and agree with us.

I make a very simple statement of truth when I say that until such particular brotherhood is practiced, universal brotherhood will remain a meaningless term. For universal brotherhood is an end, a goal, and the way to it is by particular brotherhood. The one is sublime and far-reaching consummation, the other is the means by which that consummation must be realized.

False Propagation of Brotherhood

I remember on one occasion reading a paper devoted largely to the teachings of universal brotherhood, and the leading article—a long and learned one—was an exposition of this subject. But on turning over a few more pages, I found another piece by the same writer in which he accused of misrepresentation, lying, and selfishness, not his enemies, but the brethren of his own Society, who bear, at least as far as such sins are concerned, stainless reputations.

A scriptural writer asked the question, "If a man does not love his brother whom he has seen, how can he love God whom he has not seen?" In the same manner, if a man does not love the brother whom he knows, how can he love people of all creeds and all nations whom he does not know?

To write articles on universal brotherhood is one thing; to live in peace with one's relations and neighbors and to return good for evil is quite another.

To endeavor to propagate universal brotherhood while fostering in our heart some sparks of envy, spite, and resentment, malice, or hatred, is to be self-deluded; for thus shall we be all the time hindering and denying, by our actions, that which we eulogize by our words. So subtle is such self-delusion, that, until the very heights of love and wisdom are reached, we are all liable at any moment to fall into it.

Practicing Brotherhood Here and Now

It is not because our fellow men do not hold our views, or follow our religion, or see as we see that universal brotherhood remains unrealized, but because of the prevalence of ill will. If we hate, avoid, and condemn others because they differ from us, all that we may say or do in the cause of universal brotherhood will be another snare to our feet, a mockery to our aspirations, and a farce to the world at large.

Let us, then, remove all hatred and malice from our hearts. Let us be filled with goodwill toward those who try and test us by their immediate nearness. Let us love them that hate us, and think magnanimously of those who condemn us or our doctrine—in a word, let us take the first step toward universal brotherhood, by practicing brotherhood in the place where it is most needed. And as we succeed in being brotherly in these important particulars, universal brotherhood will be found to be not far distant.

Light on Life's Sorrows

THERE IS GREAT SORROW IN THE WORLD. This is one of the supreme facts of life. Grief and affliction visit every heart, and many that are today reveling in hilarious joy or sinful riot, will tomorrow be smitten low with sorrow. Suddenly, and with swift and silent certainty, comes its poignant arrow, entering the human heart, slaying its joy, laying low its hopes, and shattering all its earthly plans and prospects. Then the humbled, smitten soul reflects, and enters deeply and sympathetically into the hidden meanings of human life.

In the dark times of sorrow, men and women approach very near to Truth. When in one brief hour the built up hopes of many years of toil fall like a toy palace, and all earthly pleasures burst and vanish like petty bubbles in the grasp, then the crushed spirit, bewildered, tempest-tossed, and without a refuge, gropes in dumb anguish for the Eternal, and seeks its abiding peace.

Sorrow Is a Blessing in Disguise

"Blessed are they that mourn," said the Teacher of the West, and the Teacher of the East declared that, "Where there is great suffering there is great bliss." Both of these sayings express the truth that sorrow is a teacher and purifier. Sorrow is not the end of life—though it is, in its consummation, the end of the worldly life—it leads the bewildered spirit into rest and safety; for the end of sorrow is joy and peace.

Strong searcher for Truth! Strenuous fighter against self and passion! Seasons of sorrow must be your portion for a time. While any vestige of self remains, temptations will assail you; the veil of illusion will cloud your spiritual vision, producing sorrow and unrest. When heavy clouds settle down upon your spirit, accept the darkness as your own, and pass through it bravely into the cloudless light beyond.

Bear well in mind t hat nothing can overtake you that does not belong to you and that is not for your eternal good. As the poet has truly sung—

Nor space nor time, nor deep nor high
Can keep my own away from me.

And not alone are the bright things of life yours;

the dark things are yours also.

Accept Your Sufferings

When difficulties and troubles gather thickly about you; when failures come and friends fall away; when the tongue that has sweetly praised you, bitterly blames; when beloved lips that pressed against your lips, the soft, warm kisses of love, taunt and mock you in the lonely hour of your solitary grief; or when you lay beneath the sod the cold casket of clay that but yesterday held the responsive spirit of your beloved—when these things overtake you, remember that the hour of your Gethsemane has come. The cup of anguish is yours to drink. Drink it silently and murmur not, for in that hour of oppressive darkness and blinding pain no prayer will save you, no cry to heaven will bring you sweet relief. Faith and patience only will give you the strength to endure, and to go through your crucifixion with a meek and gentle spirit, not complaining, blaming no one, but accepting it as your own.

Rising Above Sorrow

When one has reached the lowest point of sorrow; when, weak and exhausted, and overcome with a sense of powerlessness, he cries to God for help, and there comes no answering comfort and no relief—then, discovering the painfulness of sorrow and the insufficiency of prayer alone, he is ready to enter the path of self-renunciation, ready to purify his heart, ready to practice self-control, ready to become a spiritual athlete, and to develop that divine and invincible strength which is born of self-mastery.

He will find the cause of sorrow in his own heart, and will remove it. He will learn to stand alone; not craving sympathy from any, but giving it to all. Not thoughtlessly sinning and remorsefully repenting, but studying how not to commit sin. Humbled by innumerable defeats, and chastened by many sufferings, he will learn how to act blamelessly toward others, how to be gentle and strong, kind and steadfast, compassionate and wise.

Thus he will gradually rise above sorrow, and at last Truth will dawn upon his mind, and he will understand the meaning of abiding peace. His mental eye will be open to perceive the Cosmic Order. He will be blessed with the Vision of the Law, and will receive the Beatific Bliss.

The Wise Do Not Grieve

When the true order of things is perceived, sorrow

is transcended. When the contracted personal self, which hugs its own fleeting pleasures and broods over its own petty disappointments and dissatisfactions, is broken up and cast away, then the larger life of Truth enters the mind, bringing bliss and peace; and the Universal Will takes the place of self. The individual becomes one with humanity. He forgets self in his love for all. His sorrow is swallowed up in the bliss of Truth.

Thus when you have, by experience, entered completely into the sorrow that is never lifted from the heart of humankind; when you have reaped and eaten all the bitter fruits of your own wrong thoughts and deeds—then divine compassion for all suffering beings will be born in your heart, healing all your wounds and drying all your tears. You will rise again into a new and heavenly life, where the sting of sorrow cannot enter, for there is no self there. After the crucifixion comes the transfiguration; the sorrowless state is reached through sorrow, and "the wise do not grieve."

Ever remember this—in the midst of sin and sorrow there abides the world of Truth. Redemption is at hand. The troubled may find peace; the impure may find purity. Healing awaits the broken-hearted. The weak will be adorned with strength, and the downtrodden will be lifted up and glorified.

Light on Life's Changes

THE TENDENCY OF THINGS to advance from a lower to a higher level, and from high to higher still, is universal. The worlds exist in order that beings may experience, and by experiencing, acquire knowledge and increase in wisdom.

Evolution is only another name for progress. It signifies perpetual change, but a purposeful change, a change accompanied by growth. Evolution does not mean the creation of a new being from a being of a different order. It means the modification of beings by experience and change; and such modification is progress.

The fact of change is ever before us. Nothing can escape it. Plants, animals, and human beings germinate, reach maturity, and pass into decay. Even the lordly suns and their attendant worlds rolling through illimitable spaces, although their life is reckoned in millions of years, at last decay and perish after having passed through innumerable changes. We cannot say of any being or object—"This will remain forever as it is," for even while we are saying it, the being or object would be undergoing change.

Sadness and suffering accompany this change; and beings mourn for that which has departed, for the things which are lost and gone. Yet in reality change is good, for it is the open door to all achievement, advancement, and perfection.

Mind, as well as matter, is subject to the same change. Every experience, every thought, every deed, changes a person. There is little resemblance between the elderly and their period of childhood and youth.

An eternally fixed, unchangeable being is not known. Such a being may be assumed, but it is a postulate only. It is not within the range of human observation and knowledge. A being not subject to change would be a being outside progress.

Avoiding the Two Extremes

There is a teaching which declares that man has a spiritual soul that is eternally pure, eternally unchanged, eternally perfect, and that sinning, suffering, changing man as we see him is an illusion—

that, indeed, the spiritual soul is the man, and the other is unreality.

There is another teaching that affirms that man is eternally imperfect, that stainless purity can never be reached, and that perfection is an impossibility, an illusion.

It will be found that these two extremes have no relation to human experience. They are both of the nature of speculative metaphysics which stand in opposition to the facts of life; so much so that the adherents of these two extremes deny the existence of the commonest everyday facts of human experience. That which is assumed is regarded as real; the facts of life are declared to be unreal.

It is well to avoid both these extremes, and find the middle way of human experience. It is well to avoid opinions and speculations of our own or others, it is well to refer to the facts of life. We see that man passes through birth and growth and old age, that he experiences sin, sickness, and death; that he sorrows and suffers, aspires and rejoices; and that he is ever looking forward to greater purity and striving toward perfection. These are not opinions, speculations, or metaphysics—they are universal facts.

If man were already perfect, there would be no

need for him to be perfected, and all moral teaching would be useless and ridiculous. Moreover, a perfect being could not be subject to illusion and unreality.

On the other hand, if a man could never attain to purity and perfection, his aspirations and striving would be useless. They would indeed be mockeries; and the heavenly perfection of saintly and divine men and women would have to be belittled and denied.

We see around us sin, sorrow, and suffering; and we see before us, in the lives of the great teachers, the sinless, sorrowless, divine state. Therefore, we know that man is an imperfect being, yet capable of, and destined for, perfection. The divine state toward which he aspires, he will reach. The fact that he so ardently desires it means that he can reach it, even if the fact were not demonstrated in those great ones who have already attained.

Man is not a compound of two beings, one real and perfect, the other unreal and imperfect. He is one and real, and his experiences are real. His imperfection is apparent, and his advancement and progress are also apparent.

The realities of life claim men in spite of their metaphysics, and all come under the same law of change and progress. He who affirms the eternal sinlessness and perfection of man, should not, to be logical and consistent, ever speak of sins and faults, of disease and death; yet he refers to these things as matters to be dealt with. Thus in theory he denies the existence of that which he habitually recognizes in practice.

He also who denies the possibility of perfection should not aspire or strive; yet we find him practicing self-denial and striving ceaselessly toward perfection.

To Experience is To Change

Holding to the theoretical does not absolve one from the inevitable. The teacher of the unreality of sickness, old age, and death is at last caught in the toils of disease, succumbs to age, and disappears in death.

Change is not only inevitable; it is the constant and unvarying law. Without it, everything would remain forever as it is, and there would be neither growth nor progress.

The strenuous struggle of all life is a prophecy of its perfection. The looking upward of all beings is evidence of their ceaseless ascension. Aspirations, ideals, moral aims, while they denote man's imperfection, assuredly point to his future perfection. They are neither unnecessary nor aimless, but are woven into the fabric of things. They belong to the vital essence of the universe.

Whatsoever a man believes or disbelieves, what theories he holds or does not hold, one thing is certain—he is found in the stream of life, and must think and act. To think and act is to experience; and to experience is to change and develop.

That man is conscious of sin means that he can become pure; that he abhors evil signifies that he can reach up to Good; that he is a pilgrim in the land of error assures us, without doubt, that he will at last come to the beautiful city of Truth.

Light on the Truth of Transitoriness

IT IS WELL SOMETIMES to meditate deeply and seriously on the truth of Transitoriness. By meditation we will come to perceive how all compounded things must pass away; yea, how even while they remain they are already in the process of passing away. Such meditation will soften the heart, deepen the understanding, and render one more fully conscious of the sacred nature of life.

What is there that does not pass away, among all the things of which a man says, "This will be mine tomorrow"? Even the mind is continually changing. Old characteristics die and pass away, and new ones are formed. In the midst of life all things are dying. Nothing endures; nothing can be retained. Things appear and then disappear; they become, and then they pass away.

The ancient sages declared the visible universe to be Maya, illusion, meaning thereby that impermanency is the antithesis of Reality. Change and decay are in the very nature of visible things, and they are unreal—illusory—in the sense that they pass away forever.

The Lesson of Perishability

He who would ascend into the realm of Reality, who would penetrate into the world of Truth, must first perceive, with no uncertain vision, the transitory nature of the things of life. He must cease to delude himself into believing that he can retain his hold on his possessions, his body, his pleasures and objects of pleasure. For as the flower fades and as the leaves of the tree fall and wither, so must these things, in their season, pass away forever.

The perception of the Truth of Transitoriness is one of the few great steps in wisdom, for when it is fully grasped, and its lesson has sunk deeply into the heart, the clinging to perishable things which is the cause of all sorrow, will be yielded up, and the search for the Truth which abides will be accelerated.

Anguish is rife because men and women set their hearts on the acquisition of things that perish, because they lust for the possession of those things which even when obtained cannot be retained.

There is no sorrow that would not vanish if the clinging to transient things were given up. There is no grief that would not be dispersed if the desire to have and to hold things which in their very nature cannot endure were taken out of the heart.

Tens of thousands of grief-stricken hearts are today bewailing the loss of some loved object which they called theirs in days that are past, are weeping over that which is gone forever and cannot be restored.

Clinging to Impermanence

Men are slow to learn the lessons of experience and to acquire wisdom, and unnumbered griefs and pains and sorrows have failed to impress them with the Truth of Transitoriness. He who clings to that which is impermanent cannot escape sorrow, and the intensity of his sorrow will be measured by the strength of his clinging. He who sets his heart on perishable things embraces the companionship of grief and lamentation.

Men and women cannot find wisdom because they will not renounce the clinging to things. They believe that clinging to perishable objects is the source of happiness, and not the cause of sorrow. They cannot escape unrest and enter into the life of peace because desire is difficult to quench, and the immediate and transitory pleasure which gratified desire affords is mistaken for abiding joy.

It is because the true order of things is not understood that grief is universal. It is ignorance of the fleeting nature of things that lies at the root of sorrow.

The sting of anguish will be taken out of life when the lust to hold and to preserve the things of decay is taken out of the heart.

Sorrow is ended for him who sees things as they are; who, realizing the nature of transiency, detaches his heart and mind from the things that perish.

There is a right use for perishable things, and when they are rightly used, and not doted upon for themselves alone, their loss will cause no sorrow.

Finding Lasting Joy in Truth

If a rich man thinks in his heart, "My riches and possessions are no part of me, nor can I call them mine, seeing that when I am summoned to depart from this world, I cannot take them with me; they are entrusted to me to be used rightly, and I will employ them to the best of my ability for the good of men and for the world," such a man, though surrounded by luxuries and responsibilities, will be lifted above sorrow, and will draw near to the Truth. On the other hand, if the poor man does not covet riches and possessions, his condition will cause him no anxiety and unrest.

He who by a right understanding of life rids his heart of all selfish grasping and clinging, who uses things wisely and in their proper place, and who, with chastened heart, and mind clarified of all thirsty desires, remains serene and self-contained in the midst of all changes, such a man will find Truth. He will stand face to face with Reality.

For in the midst of all error there abides the Truth; at the heart of the transiency there reposes the Permanent; and illusion does but veil the eternal and unchanging Reality.

The nature of that Reality it is not my purpose to deal with here. Let it suffice that I indicate that it is only found by abandoning, in the heart, all that is not of Love and Compassion, Wisdom and Purity. In these things there is no element of transitoriness, no sorrow, and no unrest.

When the truth of Transitoriness is well perceived, and when the lesson contained in the truth of Transitoriness is well learned, then does a man set out to find the abiding Truth; then does he wean his heart from those selfish elements which are productive of sorrow.

He whose treasure is Truth, who fashions his life in accordance with Wisdom, will find the Joy which does not pass away. He will leave behind him the land of lamentation, and, crossing the wide ocean of illusion, will come to the Sorrowless Shore.

The Light That Never Goes Out

AMID THE MULTITUDE of conflicting opinions and theories, and caught in the struggle of existence, whither shall the confused truth-seeker turn to find the path that leads to peace unending? To what refuge shall he fly from the uncertainties and sorrows of change?

Will he find peace in pleasure? Pleasure has its place, and in its place it is good; but as an end, as a refuge, it affords no shelter. He who seeks it as such does but increase the anguish of life; for what is more fleeting than pleasure, and what is more empty than the heart that seeks satisfaction in so ephemeral a thing? There is, therefore, no abiding refuge in pleasure.

Will he find peace in wealth and worldly success?

Wealth and worldly success have their place, but they are fickle and uncertain possessions, and he who seeks them for themselves alone will be burdened with many anxieties and cares. When the storms of adversity sweep over his glittering yet frail habitation, he will find himself helpless and exposed. But even should he maintain such possessions throughout life, what satisfaction will they afford him in the hour of death? There is no abiding refuge in wealth and worldly success.

Will he find peace in health? Health has its place, and it should not be thrown away or despised, but it belongs to the body which is destined for dissolution, and is therefore perishable. Even should health be maintained for a hundred years, the time will come when the physical energies will decline and debility and decay will overtake them. There is no abiding refuge in health.

Will he find refuge in those whom he dearly loves? Those whom he loves have their place in his life. They afford him means of practicing unselfishness, and thereby arriving at Truth. He should cherish them with loving care, and consider their needs before his own. But the time will come when they will be separated from him, and he will be left alone.

There is no abiding refuge in loved ones.

Will he find peace in this Scripture or that? Scripture fills an important place. As a guide it is good, but it cannot be a refuge, for one may know the Scripture by heart, and yet be in sore conflict and unrest. The theories of men are subject to successive changes, and no limit can be set to the variety of textual interpretations. There is no abiding refuge in Scripture.

Will he find rest in this teacher or that? The teacher has his place, and as an instructor he renders good service. But teachers are numerous, and their differences are many. Though one may regard his particular teacher as in possession of the Truth, that teacher will one day be taken from him. There is no abiding refuge in a teacher.

Will he find peace in solitude? Solitude is good and necessary in its place, but he who courts it as a lasting refuge will be like one perishing of thirst in a waterless desert. He will escape men and the turmoil of the city, but he will not escape himself and the unrest of the heart. There is no abiding rest in solitude.

If, then, the seeker can find no refuge in pleasure, in success, in health, in family and friends, in Scripture, in the teacher, or in solitude, whither shall he turn to find that sanctuary which shall afford abiding peace?

Let him take refuge in righteousness. Let him fly to the sanctuary of a purified heart. Let him enter the pathway of a blameless, stainless life, and walk it meekly and patiently until it brings him to the eternal temple of Truth in his own heart.

He who has taken refuge in Truth, even in the habitation of a wise understanding and a loving and steadfast heart, is the same whether in pleasure or pain; wealth or poverty; success or failure; health or sickness; with friends or without; in solitude or noisy haunts; and he is independent of bibles and teachers, for the spirit of Truth instructs him. He perceives without fear or sorrow the change and decay which are in all things. He has found peace; he has entered the abiding sanctuary; he knows the Light that will never go out.

Lo! we are great
As we subdue ourselves and stand supreme
O'er Form and Fate;
We conquer as we yield our selfish dream
Of love and hate.

Book Two

Above Life's Turmoil

Above Life's Turmoil

Table of Contents

Foreword

WE CANNOT ALTER EXTERNAL THINGS, nor shape other people to our liking, nor mold the world to our wishes; but we can alter internal things—our desires, passions, thoughts—we can shape our liking to other people, and we can mold the inner world of our own mind in accordance with wisdom, and so reconcile it to the outer world of men and things.

The turmoil of the world we cannot avoid, but the disturbances of the mind we can overcome. The duties and difficulties of life claim our attention, but we can rise above all anxiety concerning them. Surrounded by noise, we can yet have a quiet mind; involved in responsibilities, the heart can be at rest; in the midst of strife, we can know abiding peace.

The twenty chapters which comprise this book, unrelated as some of them are in the letter, will be found to be harmonious in the spirit, in that they point the reader toward those heights of self-knowledge and self-conquest which, rising above the turbulence of the world, lift their peaks where the Heavenly Silence reigns.

—James Allen

True Happiness

TO MAINTAIN AN UNCHANGEABLE SWEETNESS of disposition, to think only thoughts that are pure and gentle, and to be happy under all circumstances—such blessed conditions and such beauty of character and life should be the aim of all, and particularly so of those who wish to lessen the misery of the world. If anyone has failed to lift himself above ungentleness, impurity, and unhappiness, he is greatly deluded if he imagines he can make the world happier by the propagation of any theory or theology. He who is daily living in harshness, impurity, or unhappiness is, day by day, adding to the sum of the world's misery. Whereas he who continually lives in good will, and does not depart from happiness is, day by day, increasing the sum of the world's happiness, and this independently of any religious beliefs which these may or may not hold.

Happiness Purifies the World

He who has not learned how to be gentle, forgiving, loving, and happy has learned very little, great though his book-learning and profound his acquaintance with the letter of Scripture may be. For it is in the process of becoming gentle, pure, and happy that the deep, real, and enduring lessons of life are learned. Unbroken sweetness of conduct in the face of all outward antagonism is the infallible indication of a self-conquered soul, the witness of wisdom, and the proof of the possession of Truth.

A sweet and happy soul is the ripened fruit of experience and wisdom, and it sheds abroad the invisible yet powerful aroma of its influence, gladdening the hearts of others, and purifying the world. And all who will, and who have not yet commenced, may begin this day, if they will so resolve, to live sweetly and happily, as becomes the dignity of true manhood and womanhood.

Do you say that your surroundings are against you? A man's surroundings are never against him. They are there to aid him, and all those outward occurrences over which you lose your sweetness and peace of mind are the very conditions necessary to your development. It is only by meeting and overcoming them that you can learn, and grow, and ripen. The fault is in yourself.

~ *Above Life's Turmoil*

Pure happiness is the rightful and healthy condition of the soul, and all may possess it if they will live purely and unselfishly:

> *Have goodwill to all that lives;*
> *Letting unkindness die,*
> *And greed and wrath,*
> *So that your lives be made*
> *Like soft airs passing by.*

Is this too difficult for you? Then unrest and unhappiness will continue to dwell in you. Your belief and aspiration and resolve are all that are necessary to make it easy, to render it in the near future a thing accomplished, a blessed state realized.

Cease To Be Pessimistic

Despondency, irritability, anxiety, complaining, condemning, and grumbling—all these are thought-cankers, mind-diseases. They are the indications of a wrong mental condition, and those who suffer therefrom would do well to remedy their thinking and conduct. It is true there is much sin and misery in the world, so that all our love and compassion are needed, but our misery is not needed—there is already too much of that. No, it is our cheerfulness and our happiness that are needed, for there is too little of that. We can give nothing better to the world than beauty of life and character; without this, all other things are vain. This is preeminently excellent; it is enduring, real, and not to be overthrown, and it includes all joy and blessedness.

Cease to dwell pessimistically upon the wrongs around you. Dwell no more in complaints about, and revolt against, the evil in others, and commence to live free from all wrong and evil yourself. Peace of mind, pure religion, and true reform lie this way. If you would have others true, be true. If you would have the world emancipated from misery and sin, emancipate yourself. If you would have your home and surroundings happy, be happy. You can transform everything around you if you will transform yourself.

Don't bewail and bemoan....
Don't waste yourself in rejection,
Nor bark against the bad,
But chant the beauties of the good.

And this you will naturally and spontaneously do as you realize the good in yourself.

The Immortal Man

IMMORTALITY IS HERE AND NOW, and is not a speculative something beyond the grave. It is a lucid state of consciousness in which the sensations of the body, the varying and unrestful states of mind, and the circumstances and events of life are seen to be of a fleeting, and therefore of an illusionary, character.

Immortality does not belong to time, and will never be found in time. It belongs to Eternity; and just as time is here and now, so is Eternity here and now. A man may find that Eternity and establish himself in it, if he will overcome the self that derives its life from the unsatisfying and perishable things of time.

While a man remains immersed in sensation, desire, and the passing events of his day-to-day existence, and regards these sensations, desires, and passing events as of the essence of himself, he can have no knowledge of immortality. The thing which such a man desires, and which he mistakes for immortality, is persistence; that is, a continuous succession of sensations and events in time. Living in, loving, and clinging to the things which stimulate and minister to his immediate gratification, and realizing no state of consciousness above and independent of this, he thirsts for its continuance. He strives to banish the thought that he will have to part from those earthly luxuries and delights to which he has been enslaved, and which he regards as being inseparable from himself.

Persistence is the antithesis of immortality; and to be absorbed in it is spiritual death. Its very nature is change, impermanence. It is a continual living and dying.

Mortal Man Thirsts for Pleasure

The death of the body can never bestow upon a man immortality. Spirits are not different from men, and live their little feverish life of broken consciousness, and are still immersed in change and mortality. The mortal man, he who thirsts for the persistence of his pleasure-loving personality, is still mortal after death, and only lives another life with a beginning and an end, without memory of the past or knowledge of the future.

The immortal man is he who has detached himself from the things of time by having ascended into that state of consciousness which is fixed and invariable, and is not affected by passing events and sensations. Human life consists of an ever-moving procession of events, and in this procession the mortal man is immersed, and he is carried along with it; and being so carried along, he has no knowledge of what is behind and before him.

Immortal Man is a Witness

The immortal man is he who has stepped out of this procession, and he stands unmoved and watches it. From his fixed place he sees both the before, the behind, and the middle of the moving thing called life. No longer identifying himself with the sensations and fluctuations of the personality, or with the outward changes which make up the life in time, he has become the passionless spectator of his own destiny and of the destinies of men and nations.

The mortal man, also, is as one who is caught in a dream, and he neither knows that he was formerly awake, nor that he will wake again. He is a dreamer without knowledge, nothing more.

The immortal man is as one who has awakened out of a dream, and he knows that his dream was not an enduring reality, but a passing illusion. He is a man with knowledge, the knowledge of both states—that of persistence, and that of immortality—and is in full possession of himself.

The mortal man lives in the time or world state of consciousness which begins and ends. The immortal man lives in the cosmic or heaven state of consciousness, in which there is neither beginning nor end, but an eternal now. Such a man remains poised and steadfast under all changes, and the death of his body will not in any way interrupt the eternal consciousness in which he abides. Of such a one it is said, "He shall not taste of death," because he has stepped out of the stream of mortality, and established himself in the abode of Truth. Bodies, personalities, nations, and worlds pass away, but Truth remains, and its glory is undimmed by time.

The immortal man, then, is he who has conquered himself. He no longer identifies himself with the self-seeking forces of the personality, but has trained himself to direct those forces with the hand of a master, and so has brought them into harmony with the causal energy and source of all things.

The fret and fever of life has ceased, doubt and fear are cast out, and death is not for him who has realized the fadeless splendor of that life of Truth by adjusting heart and mind to the eternal and unchangeable verities.

The Overcoming of Self

MANY PEOPLE have very confused and erroneous ideas concerning the terms "the overcoming of self," "the eradication of desire," and the "annihilation of the personality." Some (particularly the intellectual, who are prone to theories) regard it as a metaphysical theory altogether apart from life and conduct; while others conclude that it is the crushing out of all life, energy, and action, and the attempt to idolize stagnation and death. These errors and confusions, arising as they do in the minds of individuals, can only be removed by the individuals themselves. But perhaps it may make their removal a little less difficult (for those who are seeking Truth) by presenting the matter in another way.

The Annihilation of Self

The doctrine of the overcoming or annihilation of self is simplicity itself. Indeed, so simple, practical, and close at hand is it that a child of five, whose mind has not yet been clouded by theories, theological schemes, and speculative philosophies, would be far more likely to comprehend it than many older people who have lost their hold upon simple and beautiful truths by the adoption of complicated theories.

The annihilation of self consists in weeding out and destroying all those elements in the soul which lead to division, strife, suffering, disease, and sorrow. It does not mean the destruction of any good, beautiful, and peace-producing quality.

For instance, when a man is tempted to irritability or anger, and by a great effort overcomes the selfish tendency, casts it from him, and acts from the spirit of patience and love, in that moment of self-conquest he practices annihilation of self. Every noble man practices it in part, though he may deny it in his words. He who carries out this practice to its completion, eradicating every selfish tendency until only the divinely beautiful qualities remain, he is said to have annihilated the personality (all the personal elements) and to have arrived at Truth.

The Ten Producers of Sorrow and Divinity

The self which is to be annihilated is composed of the following ten worthless and sorrow-producing elements: lust, hatred, avarice, self-indulgence, self-seeking, vanity, pride, doubt, pessimism, and delusion. It is the total abandonment, the complete annihilation of these ten elements, for they comprise the body of desire. On the other hand, it teaches the cultivation, the practice of the following ten divine qualities: Purity, Patience, Humility, Self-Sacrifice, Self-Reliance, Fearlessness, Knowledge, Wisdom, Compassion, and Love. These comprise the Body of Truth, and to live entirely in them is to be a doer and knower of the Truth, is to be an embodiment of Truth.

The combination of the ten elements is called self or the personality. The combination of the ten qualities produces what is called Truth; the Impersonal; the abiding, real, and immortal man.

No More Selfish Longing

It will thus be seen that it is not the destruction of any noble, true, and enduring quality that is taught, but only the destruction of those things that are ignoble, false, and transitory. Neither is this overcoming of the self the deprivation of gladness, happiness, and joy, but rather it is the constant possession of these things by living in the joy-begetting qualities. It is the abandonment of the lust for enjoyment, but not of enjoyment itself; the destruction of the thirst for pleasure, but not of pleasure itself, the annihilation of the selfish longing for love, power, and possessions themselves. It is the preservation of all those things which draw and bind men together in unity and concord. Far from idealizing stagnation and death, it urges men to the practice of those qualities which lead to the highest, noblest, most effective, and most enduring action.

He whose actions proceed from some or all of the ten elements wastes his energies upon negations, and does not preserve his soul. But he whose actions proceed from some or all of the ten qualities, he truly and wisely acts and so preserves his soul.

He who lives largely in the ten earthly elements, and who is blind and deaf to the spiritual verities, will find no attraction in the doctrine of self-surrender, for it will appear to him as the complete extinction of his being. But he who is endeavoring to live the ten heavenly qualities will see the glory and beauty of the doctrine, and will know it as the foundation of Life Eternal. He will also see that when men comprehend and practice it, industry, commerce, government, and every worldly activity will be purified. And action, purpose, and intelligence, instead of being destroyed, will be intensified and enlarged, but freed from strife and pain.

The Uses of Temptation

THE SOUL, IN ITS JOURNEY towards perfection, passes through three distinct stages. The first is the *animal* stage, in which the man is content to live in the gratification of his senses, unawakened to the knowledge of sin, or of his divine inheritance, and altogether unconscious of the spiritual possibilities within himself.

The second is the *dual* stage, in which the mind is continually oscillating between the animal and divine tendencies, having become awakened to the consciousness of both. It is during this stage that temptation plays its part in the progress of the soul. It is a stage of continual fighting, of falling and rising, of sinning and repenting, for the man, still loving, and reluctant to leave, the gratifications in which he has so long lived, yet also aspires to the purity and excellence of the spiritual state, and he is continually mortified by an undecided choice.

Urged on by the divine state within him, this stage becomes at last one of deep anguish and suffering, and then the soul is ushered into the third stage, that of *knowledge*, in which one arises above sin and temptation, and enters into peace.

Temptation is Transient

Temptation, like contentment in sin, is not a lasting condition, as the majority of people suppose. It is a passing phase, an experience through which the soul must pass. But as to whether a man will pass through that condition in this present life, and realize holiness and heavenly rest here and now, will depend entirely upon the strength of his intellectual and spiritual exertions, and upon the intensity and enthusiasm with which he searches for Truth.

Temptation, with all its attendant torments, can be overcome here and now, but it can only be overcome with knowledge. It is a condition of darkness, or of semi-darkness. The fully enlightened soul is proof against all temptation. When a man fully understands the source, nature, and meaning of temptation, in that hour he will conquer it, and will rest from his long travail. But while he remains in ignorance, attention to religious observances, and much praying and reading of Scripture will fail to bring him peace.

Watchfulness of the Inner Enemy

If a man goes out to conquer an enemy, knowing nothing of his enemy's strength, tactics, or place of ambush, he will not only disgracefully fail, but will speedily fall into the hands of the enemy. He who would overcome his enemy, the tempter, must discover his stronghold and place of concealment, and must find out the unguarded gates in his own fortress where his enemy effects so easy entrance. This necessitates continual meditation, ceaseless watchfulness, and constant and rigid introspection which lays bare, before the spiritual eyes of the tempted, the vain and selfish motives of his soul. This is the holy war of the saints. It is the fight upon which every soul enters when it awakens out of its long sleep of animal indulgence.

Delusion Must Be Replaced with Truth

Men fail to conquer, and the fight is indefinitely prolonged, because they labor, almost universally, under two delusions: first, that all temptations come from without; and second, that they are tempted because of their goodness. While a man is held in bondage by these two delusions, he will make no progress. When he has shaken them off, he will pass on rapidly from victory to victory, and will taste of spiritual joy and rest.

Two searching truths must take the place of these two delusions, and these truths are: first, that all temptation comes from within; and second, that a man is tempted because of the evil that is within him. The idea that God, a devil, evil spirits, or outward objects are the source of temptation must be dispelled.

The source and cause of all temptation is the inward desire; that being purified or eliminated, outward objects and extraneous powers are utterly powerless to move the soul to sin or temptation. The outward object is merely the occasion of the temptation, never the cause; this is in the desire of the one tempted. If the cause existed in the object, everyone would be tempted alike, temptation would never be overcome, and everyone would be helplessly doomed to endless torment. But seated, as it is, in one's own desires, everyone has the remedy in his or her own hands, and can become victorious over all temptation by purifying those desires.

Goodness Destroys Temptation

A man is tempted because there are within him certain desires or states of mind which he has come to regard as unholy. These desires may lie asleep for a long time, and a man may think that he has got rid of them, when suddenly, on the presentation of an outward object, the sleeping desire wakes up and thirsts for immediate gratification; and this is the state of temptation.

The good in man is never tempted. Goodness destroys temptation. It is the evil in man that is aroused and tempted. The measure of a man's temptations is the exact register of his own unholiness. As a man purifies his heart, temptation ceases. For when a certain unlawful desire has been taken out of the heart, the object which formerly appealed to it can no longer do so, but becomes dead and powerless, for there is nothing left in the heart that can respond to it.

The honest man cannot be tempted to steal, let the occasion be ever so opportune. The man of purified appetites cannot be tempted to gluttony and drunkenness, though foods and wines be the most luscious. He of an enlightened understanding, whose mind is calm in the strength of inward virtue, can never be tempted to anger, irritability, or revenge, and the wiles and charms of the wanton fall upon the purified heart as empty meaningless shadows.

The Soul Grows by Temptation

Temptation shows a man just where he is sinful and ignorant, and is the means of urging him on to the higher attitudes of knowledge and purity. Without temptation the soul could not grow and become strong, there could be no wisdom, no real virtue. And though there would be lethargy and death, there would be no peace and fullness of life.

When temptation is understood and conquered, perfection is assured, and such perfection may become any man's who is willing to cast every selfish and impure desire by which he is possessed into the sacrificial fire of knowledge. Let men, therefore, search diligently for Truth, realizing that while they are subject to temptation, they have not comprehended the Truth, and have much to learn.

You who are tempted, know, then, that you are tempted of yourselves. "For every man is tempted when he is drawn away of his own lusts," says the apostle James. You are tempted because you are clinging to the animal within you and are unwilling to let go; because you are living in that false mortal self which is ever devoid of all true knowledge, knowing nothing, seeking nothing but its own immediate gratification, ignorant of every Truth, and of every divine Principle.

Clinging to that self, you continually suffer the pains of three separate torments: the torment of desire, the torment of repletion, and the torment of remorse. In that false self lies the germ of every suffering, the blight of every hope, the substance of every grief.

When you are ready to give it up; when you are willing to have laid bare before you all its selfishness, impurity, and ignorance, and to confess its darkness to the uttermost, then will you enter upon the life of self-knowledge and self-mastery. You will become conscious of the God within you, of that divine nature which, seeking no gratification, abides in a region of perpetual joy and peace where suffering cannot come, and where temptation can find no foothold.

Establishing yourself, day by day, more and more firmly in that inward Divinity, the time will at last come when you will be able to say with Him whom millions worship, few understand, and fewer still follow—"The Prince of this world cometh and hath nothing in me."

The Man of Integrity

THERE ARE TIMES IN THE LIFE of every man, who takes his stand on high moral principles, where his faith in, and knowledge of, those principles is tested to the uttermost. The way in which he comes out of the fiery trial decides whether he has sufficient strength to live as a man of Truth, and join the company of the free, or shall still remain a slave and a hireling to the cruel taskmaster, Self.

Such times of trial generally assume the form of temptation to do a wrong thing and continue in comfort and prosperity, or to stand by what is right and accept poverty and failure. So powerful is the trial that, to the tempted one, it plainly appears on the face of things as though, if he chooses the wrong, his material success will be assured for the remainder of his life, but if he does what is right, he will be ruined forever.

Frequently, the man at once loses courage and

gives way before this appalling prospect which the Path of Righteousness seems to hold out for him. But should he prove sufficiently strong to withstand this onslaught of temptation, then the inward seducer, the spirit of self, assumes the garb of an Angel of Light, and whispers, "Think of your wife and children. Think of those who are dependent upon you. Will you bring them down to disgrace and starvation?"

Strong indeed and pure must be the man who can come triumphant out of such a trial, but he who does so enters at once a higher realm of life, where his spiritual eyes are opened to see beautiful things. The poverty and ruin which seemed inevitable do not come, but a more abiding success comes, as well as a peaceful heart and a quiet conscience. But he who fails does not obtain the promised prosperity, and his heart is restless and his conscience troubled.

The right-doer cannot ultimately fail, the wrong-doer cannot ultimately succeed, for

Such is the law which moves to Righteousness
Which none at last can turn aside or stay.

It is because justice is at the heart of things—because the Great Law is good—that the man of integrity is superior to fear, and failure, and poverty, and shame, and disgrace. As the poet further says of this Law:

> *The heart of it is Love, the end of it*
> *Is peace and consummation sweet—obey.*

The man who, fearing the loss of present pleasures or material comforts, denies the Truth within him can be injured, robbed, degraded, and trampled upon because he has first injured, robbed, degraded, and trampled upon his own nobler self. But the man of steadfast virtue, of unblemished integrity, cannot be subject to such conditions, because he has denied the spineless self within him and has taken refuge in the Truth. It is not the scourge and the chains which make a man a slave, but the fact that he is a slave.

Integrity Cannot Be Subdued

Slander, accusation, and malice cannot affect the righteous man, nor call from him any bitter response. Nor does he need to go about and defend himself and prove his innocence. His innocence and integrity alone are a sufficient answer to all that hatred may attempt against him. Nor can he ever be subdued by the forces of darkness, having subdued all those forces within himself. Instead he turns all evil things to good account—out of darkness, he brings light, out of hatred love, out of dishonor honor. Slanders, envies, and misrepresentations only serve to make more bright the jewel of Truth within him, and to glorify his high and holy destiny.

Let the man of integrity rejoice and be glad when he is severely tried. Let him be thankful that he has been given an opportunity of proving his loyalty to the noble principles which he has espoused. Let him think, "Now is the hour of holy opportunity! Now is the day of triumph for Truth! Though I lose the whole world I will not desert the right!" So thinking, he will return good for evil, and will think compassionately of the wrongdoer.

The slanderer, the backbiter, and the wrong-doer may seem to succeed for a time, but the Law of Justice prevails. The man of integrity may seem to fail for a time, but he is invincible, and in none of the worlds, visible or invisible, can there be forged a weapon that shall prevail against him.

Discrimination

THERE IS ONE QUALITY which is preeminently necessary to spiritual development, the quality of discrimination.

A man's spiritual progress will be painfully slow and uncertain until there opens within him the eye of discrimination. For without this testing, proving, searching quality, he will be unable to distinguish the real from the unreal and the shadow from the substance. He will so confuse the false with the true as to mistake the inward promptings of his animal nature for those of the spirit of Truth.

A blind man left in a strange place may grope his way in darkness, but not without much confusion and many painful falls and bruising. Without discrimination a man is mentally blind, and his life is a painful groping in darkness. He lives in a confusion in which vice and virtue are indistinguishable from one another, where facts are confounded with truths, opinions with principles, and where ideas, events, men, and things appear to be out of all relation to each other.

Mind Is Developed by Use

A man's mind and life should be free from confusion. He should be prepared to meet every mental, material, and spiritual difficulty. He should not be inextricably caught (as many are) in the meshes of doubt, indecision, and uncertainty when troubles and so-called misfortunes come along. He should be fortified against every emergency that can come against him. But such mental preparedness and strength cannot be attained in any degree without discrimination, and discrimination can only be developed by bringing into play and constantly exercising the analytical faculty.

Mind, like muscle, is developed by use, and the assiduous exercise of the mind in any given direction will develop, in that direction, mental capacity and power. The merely critical faculty is developed and strengthened by continuously comparing and analyzing the ideas and opinions of others. But discrimination is something more and greater than criticism. It is a spiritual quality from which the cruelty and egotism which so frequently accompany criticism are eliminated, and by virtue of which a man sees things as they are, and not as he would like them to be.

Question Every Opinion

Discrimination, being a spiritual quality, can only be developed by spiritual methods, namely, by questioning, examining, and analyzing one's own ideas, opinions, and conduct. The critical, fault-finding faculty must be withdrawn from its merciless application to the opinions and conduct of others, and must be applied, with undiminished severity, to oneself. A man must be prepared to question his every opinion, his every thought, his every line of conduct, and rigorously and logically test them. Only in this way can the discrimination which destroys confusion be developed.

Before a man can enter upon such a mental exercise, he must make himself of a teachable spirit. This does not mean that he must allow himself to be led by others. It means that he must be prepared to yield up any cherished thought to which he clings if it will not bear the penetrating light of reason, if it shrivels up before the pure flames of searching aspirations.

The man who says, "I am right!" and who refuses to question his position in order to discover whether he is right will continue to follow the line of his passions and prejudices, and will not acquire discrimination.

The man who humbly asks, "Am I right?" and then proceeds to test and prove his position by earnest thought and the love of Truth will always be able to discover the true and to distinguish it from the false, and he will acquire the priceless possession of discrimination.

Prove All Things

The man who is afraid to think searchingly upon his opinions, and to reason critically upon his position, will have to develop moral courage before he can acquire discrimination.

A man must be true to himself, fearless with himself, before he can perceive the pure principles of Truth, before he can receive the all-revealing Light of Truth.

The more Truth is inquired of, the brighter it shines; it cannot suffer under examination and analysis.

The more error is questioned, the darker it grows; it cannot survive the entrance of pure and searching thought.

To "prove all things" is to find the good and to throw away the evil.

He who reasons and meditates learns to discriminate; he who discriminates discovers the eternally True.

Harmony, blessedness, and the Light of Truth attend upon the thoughtful.

Passion and prejudice are blind, and cannot discriminate: they are still crucifying the Christ and releasing Barabbas.

Belief: The Basis of Action

BELIEF IS AN IMPORTANT WORD in the teachings of the wise, and it figures prominently in all religions. According to Jesus, a certain kind of belief is necessary to salvation or regeneration. Buddha definitely taught that right belief is the first and most essential step in the Way of Truth, as without right belief there cannot be right conduct, and he who has not learned how to rightly govern and conduct himself has not yet comprehended the simplest rudiments of Truth.

Belief as laid down by the Great Teachers is not belief in any particular school, philosophy, or religion, but consists of an attitude of mind determining the whole course of one's life. Belief and conduct are, therefore, inseparable, for the one determines the other.

Belief is the basis of all action, and, this being so, the belief which dominates the heart or mind is shown in the life. Every man acts, thinks, and lives in exact accordance with the belief which is rooted in his innermost being. Such is the mathematical nature of the laws which govern mind that it is absolutely impossible for anyone to believe in two opposing conditions at the same time. For instance, it is impossible to believe in justice and injustice, hatred and love, peace and strife, self and truth. Every man believes in one or the other of these opposites, never in both, and the daily conduct of every man indicates the nature of his belief.

The man who believes in justice, who regards it as an eternal and indestructible Principle, never boils over with righteous indignation. He does not grow cynical and pessimistic over the inequalities of life, and remains calm and untroubled through all trials and difficulties. It is impossible for him to act otherwise, for he believes that justice reigns, and that, therefore, all that is called injustice is fleeting and illusory.

The man who is continually getting enraged over the injustice of his fellow men, who talks about himself being badly treated, or who mourns over the lack of justice in the world around him, shows by his conduct, his attitude of mind, that he believes in injustice. However he may protest to the contrary, in his innermost heart he believes that confusion and chaos are dominant in the universe, the result being that he dwells in misery and unrest, and his conduct is faulty.

Again, he who believes in love, in its stability and power, practices it under all circumstances, never deviates from it, and bestows it alike upon enemies as upon friends. He who slanders and condemns, who speaks despairingly of others, or regards them with contempt, believes not in love, but hatred. All his actions prove it, even though with tongue or pen he may eulogize love.

A Believer in Truth Does Not Suffer

The believer in peace is known by his peaceful conduct. It is impossible for him to engage in strife. If attacked, he does not retaliate, for he has seen the majesty of the angel of peace, and he can no longer pay homage to the demon of strife. The stirrer-up of strife, the lover of argument, he who rushes into self-defense upon any or every provocation, believes in strife, and will have naught to do with peace.

Further, he who believes in Truth renounces himself—that is, he refuses to center his life in those passions, desires, and characteristics which crave only their gratification. By thus renouncing, he becomes steadfastly fixed in Truth, and lives a wise, beautiful, and blameless life. The believer in self is known by his daily indulgences, gratifications, and vanities, and by the disappointments, sorrows, and mortifications which he continually suffers.

The believer in Truth does not suffer, for he has given up that self which is the cause of such suffering.

It will be seen by the foregoing that every person believes either in permanent and eternal Principles directing human life toward law and harmony, or in the negation of those Principles, with the resultant chaos in human affairs, and in his own life.

What is Right Belief?

Belief in the divine principles of Justice, Compassion, and Love constitutes the right belief laid down by Buddha as being the basis of right conduct, and also the belief in salvation as emphasized in the Christian Scriptures. For he who so believes cannot do otherwise than build his whole life upon these Principles, and so he purifies his heart, and perfects his life.

Belief in the negation of these divine Principles constitutes what is called in all religions unbelief, and this unbelief is manifested as a sinful, troubled and imperfect life.

Where there is right belief there is a blameless

and perfect life. Where there is false belief there is sin, there is sorrow, the mind and life are improperly governed, and there is affliction and unrest. "By their fruits ye shall know them."

There is much talk about "belief in Jesus," but what does belief in Jesus mean? It means belief in his words, in the Principles he enunciated—and lived, in his commandments, and in his exemplary life of perfection.

He who declares belief in Jesus, and yet is all the time living in his lusts and indulgences, or in the spirit of hatred and condemnation, is self-deceived. He believes not in Jesus. He believes in his own animal self. As a faithful servant delights in carrying out the commands of his master, so he who believes in Jesus carries out his commandments, and so is saved from sin.

The supreme test of belief in Jesus is this: Do I keep his commandments? And this test is applied by St. John himself in the following words: "He that saith, I know him (Jesus), and keepeth not his commandments, is a liar, and the truth is not in him. But whoso keepeth his word, in him verily is the word of God perfected."

You Are Saved by the Belief in Truth

It will be found, after a rigid and impartial

analysis, that belief lies at the root of all human conduct. Every thought, every act, every habit, is the direct outcome of a certain fixed belief, and one's conduct alters only as one's beliefs are modified. What we cling to, in that we believe. When our belief in a thing ceases, we can no longer cling to or practice it. It falls away from us as a garment outworn.

Men cling to their lusts, lies, and vanities, because they believe in them, believe there is gain and happiness in them. When they transfer their belief to the divine qualities of purity and humility, these sins trouble them no more.

Men are saved from error by belief in the supremacy of truth. They are saved from sin by belief in Holiness or Perfection. They are saved from evil by belief in Good, for every belief is manifested in this life.

It is not necessary to inquire as to a person's theological belief, for that is of little or no account. What can it avail one to believe that Jesus died for him or her, or that Jesus is God, or that one is "justified by faith," if that person continues to live in a lower, sinful nature? All that is necessary to ask is this: "How does one live?" "How does one conduct himself or herself under trying circumstances?" The answer to these questions will show whether one believes in the power of evil or in the power of Good.

He who believes in the power of Good lives a good, spiritual, or godly life, for Goodness is God, yea, verily, is God Himself. He will soon leave behind all his sins and sorrows who believes, with steadfast and unwavering faith, in the Supreme Good.

The Belief That Saves

IT HAS BEEN SAID that man's whole life and character is the outcome of his belief, and also that his belief has nothing to do with his life. Both statements are true. The confusion and contradiction of these two statements are only apparent, and are quickly dispelled when it is remembered that there are two entirely distinct kinds of belief, namely, Head-belief and Heart-belief.

Head, or intellectual belief, is not fundamental and causative, but is superficial and consequent. That it has no power in the molding of one's character, the most superficial observer may easily see. Take, for instance, half a dozen people from any creed. They not only hold the same theological belief, but confess the same articles of faith in every particular, and yet their characters are vastly different. One will be just as noble as another is ignoble. One will be mild and gentle, another coarse and cantankerous. One will be honest, another dishonest. One will indulge certain habits which another will rigidly renounce, and so on, plainly indicating that theological belief is not an influential factor in one's life.

A man's theological belief is merely his intellectual opinion or view of the universe, God, the Bible, etc.. But behind and underneath this head-belief there lies deeply rooted his innermost being, the hidden, silent, secret belief of his heart, and it is this belief which molds and makes his whole life. It is this which makes those six people who, while holding the same theology, are yet so vastly at variance in their deeds—they differ in the vital belief of the heart.

Heart Belief

What, then, is heart-belief?

It is that which a man loves and clings to and fosters in his soul. For he thus loves and clings to and fosters certain things in his heart, because he believes in them, and believing and loving them, he practices them. Thus is his life the effect of his belief, but it has no relation to the particular creed which comprises his intellectual belief.

One man clings to impure and immoral things because he believes in them; another does not cling to them because he has ceased to believe in them. One cannot cling to anything unless he or she believes in it. Belief always precedes action; therefore, one's deeds and life are the fruits of belief.

The Priest and the Levite who passed by the injured and helpless man held, no doubt, very strongly to the theological doctrines of their fathers—that was their intellectual belief—but in their hearts they did not believe in mercy, and so lived and acted accordingly. The good Samaritan may or may not have had any theological beliefs, nor was it necessary that he should have; but in his heart he believed in mercy, and acted accordingly.

Strictly speaking, there are only two beliefs which vitally affect the life, and they are, belief in good and belief in evil.

People who believe in all things that are good will love them, and live them. People who believe in those things that are impure and selfish will love them, and cling to them. The tree is known by its fruits.

Your belief about God, Jesus, and the Bible are one thing; your life as bound up in your actions is another. Therefore, your theological belief is of no consequence; but the thoughts which you harbor, your attitude of mind towards others, and your actions, these, and these only, determine and demonstrate whether the belief of your heart is fixed in the false or in the true.

Thought and Action

AS THE FRUIT TO THE TREE and the water to the spring, so is action to thought. It does not come into manifestation suddenly and without a cause. It is the result of a long and silent growth; the end of a hidden process which has long been gathering force. The fruit of the tree and the water gushing from the rock are both the effect of a combination of natural processes in air and earth which have long worked together in secret to produce the phenomenon. The beautiful acts of enlightenment and the dark deeds of sin are both the ripened effects of trains of thought which have long been harboring in the mind.

The sudden falling, when greatly tempted, into some grievous sin by one who was believed, and who probably believed himself, to stand firm, is seen neither to be a sudden nor a causeless thing when the hidden processes of thought, which led up to it, are revealed. The falling was merely the end, the outworking, the finished product of what commenced in the mind probably years before. The man had allowed a wrong thought to enter his mind; and a second and a third time he had welcomed it, and allowed it to nestle in his heart. Gradually he became accustomed to it, and cherished, fondled, and tended it. So it grew, until at last it attained such strength and force that it attracted to itself the opportunity which enabled it to burst forth and ripen into act.

As falls the stately building whose foundations have been gradually undermined by the action of water, so at last falls the strong man who allows corrupt thoughts to creep into his mind and secretly undermine his character.

We Are a Product of Thought

When it is seen that all sin and temptation are the natural outcome of the thoughts of the individual, the way to overcome sin and temptation becomes plain, and its achievement a near possibility, and, sooner or later, a certain reality. For if you will admit, cherish, and brood upon thoughts that are pure and good, those thoughts, just as surely as the impure, will grow and gather force, and will at last attract to themselves the opportunities which will enable them to ripen into act.

"There is nothing that shall not be revealed," and every thought that is harbored in the mind must, by virtue of the impelling force which is inherent in the universe, at last blossom into act, good or bad according to its nature. The divine Teacher and the sensualist are both the product of their own thoughts, and have become what they are as the result of the seeds of thought which they have implanted, or allowed to fall, into the garden of the heart, and have afterwards watered, tended, and cultivated.

Let no one think you can overcome sin and temptation by wrestling with opportunity; you can only overcome them by purifying your thoughts. If you will, day by day, in the silence of your soul, and in the performance of your duties strenuously overcome all erroneous inclination, and put in its place thoughts that are true and that will endure the light, opportunity to do evil will give place to opportunity for accomplishing good. For you can only attract to you that which is in harmony with your nature, and no temptation can gravitate to you unless there is that in your heart which is capable of responding to it.

Guard well your thoughts, reader, for what you

really are in your secret thoughts today, be it good or evil, you will, sooner or later, become in actual deed.

He who unwearyingly guards the portals of his mind against the intrusion of sinful thoughts, and occupies himself with loving thoughts, with pure, strong, and beautiful thoughts, will, when the season of their ripening comes, bring forth the fruits of gentle and holy deeds, and no temptation that can come against him shall find him unarmed or unprepared.

Your Mental Attitude

AS A BEING OF THOUGHT, your dominant mental attitude will determine your condition in life. It will also be the gauge of your knowledge and the measure of your attainment. The so-called limitations of your nature are the boundary lines of your thoughts. They are self-erected fences, and can be drawn to a narrower circle, extended to a wider, or be allowed to remain.

You are the thinker of your thoughts and as such you are the maker of your self and condition. Thought is causal and creative, and appears in your character and life in the form of results. There are no accidents in your life. Both its harmonies and antagonisms are the responsive echoes of your thoughts. A man thinks, and his life appears.

If your dominant mental attitude is peaceable and lovable, bliss and blessedness will follow you. If it be resistant and hateful, trouble and distress will cloud your pathway. Out of ill-will will come grief and disaster; out of good-will, healing and reparation.

You imagine your circumstances as being separate from yourself, but they are intimately related to your thought world. Nothing appears without an adequate cause. Everything that happens is just. Nothing is fated, everything is formed.

As you think, you travel; as you love, you attract. You are today where your thoughts have brought you; you will be tomorrow where your thoughts take you. You cannot escape the result of your thoughts, but you can endure and learn, can accept and be glad.

You will always come to the place where your love (your most abiding and intense thought) can receive its measure of gratification. If your love be base, you will come to a base place; if it be beautiful, you will come to a beautiful place.

All Things Await Your Acceptance

You can alter your thoughts, and so alter your condition. Strive to perceive the vastness and grandeur of your responsibility. You are powerful, not powerless. You are as powerful to obey as you are to disobey; as strong to be pure as to be impure; as ready for wisdom as for ignorance. You can learn what you will, can remain as ignorant as you choose. If you love knowledge you will obtain it; if you love wisdom you will secure it; if you love purity you will realize it. All things await your acceptance, and you choose by the thoughts which you entertain.

A man remains ignorant because he loves ignorance, and chooses ignorant thoughts. A man becomes wise because he loves wisdom, and chooses wise thoughts. No man is hindered by another; he is only hindered by himself. No man suffers because of another; he suffers only because of himself. By the noble Gateway of Pure Thought you can enter the highest Heaven; by the ignoble doorway of impure thought you can descend into the lowest hell.

Your mental attitude toward others will faithfully react upon yourself, and will manifest itself in every relation of your life. Every impure and selfish thought that you send out comes back to you in your circumstances in some form of suffering. Every pure and unselfish thought returns to you in some form of blessedness.

Your circumstances are effects of which the cause is inward and invisible. As the mother-father of your thoughts, you are the maker of your state and condition. When you know yourself you will perceive that every event in your life is weighed in the faultless balance of equity. When you understand the law within your mind you will cease to regard yourself as the impotent and blind tool of circumstances, and will become the strong and seeing master.

Sowing and Reaping

GO INTO THE FIELDS and country lanes in the springtime, and you will see farmers and gardeners busy sowing seeds in the newly prepared soil. If you were to ask any of these gardeners or farmers what kind of produce he expected from the seed he was sowing, he would doubtless regard you as foolish. He would tell you that he does not "expect" at all, that it is common knowledge that his produce will be of the kind which he is sowing, and that he is sowing wheat, or barley, or turnips, as the case may be, in order to reproduce that particular crop.

Every fact and process of Nature contain a moral lesson for the wise man. There is no law in the world of Nature around which is not to be found operating the same mathematical certainty as in the mind of man and in human life. All the parables of Jesus are illustrative of this truth, and are drawn from the simple facts of Nature. There is a process of seed-sowing in the mind and life, a spiritual sowing which leads to a harvest according to the kind of seed sown. Thoughts, words, and acts are seeds sown, and, by the inviolable law of things, they produce after their kind.

The man who thinks hateful thoughts brings hatred upon himself. The man who thinks loving thoughts is loved. The man whose thoughts, words, and acts are sincere is surrounded by sincere friends; the insincere man is surrounded by insincere friends. The man who sows wrong thoughts and deeds, and prays that God will bless him, is in the position of a farmer who, having sown weeds, asks God to bring forth for him a harvest of wheat.

That which ye sow, ye reap;
See yonder fields—
The sesame was sesame,
The corn was corn;
The silence and the darkness knew;
So is a man's fate born.
He cometh reaper of things he sowed.

He who would be blessed, let him scatter blessings. He who would be happy, let him consider the happiness of others.

Bringing Forth Abundance

Then there is another side to this seed sowing. The farmer must scatter all his seed upon the land, and then leave it to the elements. Were he to covetously hoard his seed, he would lose both it and his produce, for his seed would perish. It perishes when he sows it, but in perishing it brings forth a greater abundance.

So in life, we get by giving; we grow rich by scattering. The man who says he is in possession of knowledge which he cannot give out because the world is incapable of receiving it, either does not possess such knowledge, or, if he does, will soon be deprived of it—if he is not already so deprived. To hoard is to lose; to exclusively retain is to be dispossessed.

Even the man who would increase his material wealth must be willing to part with (invest) what little capital he has, and then wait for the increase. So long as he retains his hold on his precious money, he will not only remain poor, but will be growing poorer every day. He will, after all, lose the thing he loves, and will lose it without increase. But if he wisely lets its go; if, like the farmer, he scatters his seeds of gold, then he can faithfully wait for, and reasonably expect, the increase.

What Seeds Are You Sowing?

Men are asking God to give them peace and purity, and righteousness and blessedness, but are not obtaining these things. And why not? Because they are not practicing them, not sowing them. I once heard a preacher pray very earnestly for forgiveness, and shortly afterwards, in the course of his sermon, he called upon his congregation to "show no mercy to the enemies of the church." Such self-delusion is pitiful, and men have yet to learn that the way to obtain peace and blessedness is to scatter peaceful and blessed thoughts, words, and deeds.

Men believe that they can sow the seeds of strife, impurity, and unbrotherliness, and then gather in a rich harvest of peace, purity, and goodwill by merely asking for it. What more pathetic sight than to see an irritable and quarrelsome man praying for peace? Men reap that which they sow, and any man can reap all blessedness now and at once, if he will put aside selfishness, and sow broadcast the seeds of kindness, gentleness, and love.

If a man is troubled, perplexed, sorrowful, or unhappy, let him ask:

> "What mental seeds have I been sowing?"
> "What have I done for others?"
> "What is my attitude towards others?"
> "What seeds of trouble and sorrow have I sown that I should thus reap these bitter weeds?"

Let him seek within and find, and having found, let him abandon all the seeds of self, and sow, henceforth, only the seeds of Truth.

Let him learn of the farmer the simple truths of wisdom.

The Reign of Law

THE LITTLE PARTY GODS have had their day. The arbitrary gods, creatures of human caprice and ignorance, are falling into disrepute. Men have quarreled over and defended them until they have grown weary of the strife, and now, everywhere, they are relinquishing and breaking up these helpless idols of their worship.

The god of revenge, hatred, and jealousy, who gloats over the downfall of his enemies; the partial god who gratifies all our narrow and selfish desires; the god who saves only the creatures of his particular and special creed; the god of exclusiveness and favoritism; such were the gods (miscalled by us) of our soul's infancy, gods base and foolish as ourselves, the fabrications of our selfish self. And we relinquished our petty gods with bitter tears and misgivings, and broke our idols with bleeding hands. But in doing so, we did not lose sight of God; nay, we drew nearer to the great, silent Heart of Love.

Destroying the idols of self, we begin to comprehend somewhat of the Power which cannot be destroyed. We enter into a wider knowledge of the God of Love, of Peace, of Joy; the God in whom revenge and partiality cannot exist; the God of Light, from whose Presence the darkness of fear and doubt and selfishness cannot choose but flee.

The God of Law

We have reached some of those epochs in the world's progress which witness the passing of the false gods; the gods of human selfishness and human illusion. The new-old revelation of one universal impersonal Truth has again dawned upon the world, and its searching light has carried consternation to the perishable gods who take shelter under the shadow of self.

Men have lost faith in a god who can be cajoled, who rules arbitrarily and capriciously, subverting the whole order of things to gratify the wishes of his worshippers. They are turning with a new light in their eyes and a new joy in their hearts, to the God of Law.

And to Him they turn, not for personal happiness and gratification, but for knowledge, for understanding, for wisdom, for liberation from the bondage of self. And thus turning, they do not seek in vain, nor are they sent away empty and bewildered. They find within themselves the reign of Law, that every thought, every impulse, every act and word brings about a result in exact accordance with its own nature. They find that thoughts of love bring about beautiful and blissful conditions, that hateful thoughts bring about distorted and painful conditions, that thoughts and acts, both good and evil, are weighed in the faultless balance of the Supreme Law, and receive their equal measure of blessedness on the one hand, and misery on the other.

And thus finding, they enter a new Path, the Path of obedience to the Law. Entering that Path they no longer accuse, no longer doubt, nor fret and despond, for they know now that God is right, the universal laws are right, the cosmos is right. They know that they themselves are wrong, if wrong there is, and that their salvation depends upon themselves, upon their efforts, upon their personal acceptance of that which is good, and deliberate rejection of that which is evil. No longer merely hearers, they become doers of the Word, and they acquire knowledge, they receive understanding, they grow in wisdom, and they enter into the glorious life of liberation from the bondage of self.

Perfection Is Yours Now

"The Law of the Lord is perfect, enlightening the eyes." Imperfection lies in man's ignorance, in man's blind folly. Perfection, which is knowledge of the Perfect Law, is ready for all who earnestly seek it. It belongs to the order of things. It is yours and mine now if we will only put self-seeking on one side, and adopt the life of self-obliteration.

The knowledge of Truth, with its unspeakable joy, its calmness and quiet strength, is not for those who persist in clinging to their "rights," defending their "interests," and fighting for their "opinions"; whose works are imbued with the personal "I," and who build upon the shifting sands of selfishness and egotism. It is for those who renounce these causes of strife, these sources of pain and sorrow; and they are, indeed, Children of Truth, disciples of the Master, worshippers of the Most High.

The Children of Truth are in the world today. They are thinking, acting, writing, speaking; yea, even prophets are among us, and their influence is pervading the whole earth. An undercurrent of holy joy is gathering force in the world, so that men and women are moved with new aspirations and hopes, and even those who neither see nor hear, feel within themselves strange yearnings after a better and fuller life.

The Law reigns, and it reigns in men's hearts and lives; and they have come to understand the reign of Law who have sought out the tabernacle of the true God by the fair pathway of unselfishness.

God does not alter for man, for this would mean that the perfect must become imperfect. Man must alter for God, and this implies that the imperfect must become perfect. The law cannot be broken for man, otherwise confusion would ensue. Man must obey the Law: this is in accordance with harmony, order, justice.

The Law of Love and Law Are One

There is no more painful bondage than to be at the mercy of one's inclinations; no greater liberty than utmost obedience to the law of Being. And the Law is that the heart shall be purified, the mind regenerated, and the whole being brought in subjection to Love till self is dead and Love is all in all, for the reign of Law is the reign of Love. And Love waits for all, rejecting none. Love may be claimed and entered into now, for it is the heritage of all.

Ah, beautiful Truth! To know that now man may enter the Kingdom of Heaven!

Oh, pitiful error! To know that man rejects it because of love of self!

Obedience to the Law means the destruction of sin and self, and the realization of unclouded joy and undying peace.

Clinging to one's selfish inclinations means the drawing about one's soul clouds of pain and sorrow which darken the light of Truth; the shutting out of oneself from all real blessedness; for "whatsoever a man sows, that shall he also reap."

Verily, the Law reigneth, and reigneth forever, and Justice and Love are its eternal ministers.

The Supreme Justice

THE MATERIAL UNIVERSE is maintained and preserved by the equilibrium of its forces. The moral universe is sustained and protected by the perfect balance of its equivalents.

As in the physical world Nature abhors a vacuum, so in the spiritual world disharmony is annulled.

Underlying the disturbances and destructions of Nature, and behind the mutability of its forms, there abides the eternal and perfect mathematical symmetry. And at the heart of life, behind all its pain, uncertainty, and unrest, there abide the eternal harmony, the unbroken peace, and inviolable Justice.

Is there then no injustice in the universe? There is injustice, and there is not. It depends upon the kind of life and the state of consciousness from which a man looks out upon the world and judges. The man who lives in his passions sees injustice everywhere. The man who has overcome his passions sees the operation of Justice in every department of human life.

Injustice is the confused, feverish dream of passion, real enough to those who are dreaming it. Justice is the permanent reality in life, gloriously visible to those who have wakened out of the painful nightmare of self.

Passion Must Be Transcended

The Divine Order cannot be perceived until passion and self are transcended. The Faultless Justice cannot be apprehended until all sense of injury and wrong is consumed in the pure flames of all-embracing Love.

The man who thinks, "I have been slighted, I have been injured, I have been insulted, I have been treated unjustly," cannot know what Justice is. Blinded by self, he cannot perceive the pure Principles of Truth, and, brooding upon his wrongs, he lives in continual misery.

In the region of passion there is ceaseless conflict of forces causing suffering to all who are involved in them. There is action and reaction, deed and consequence, cause and effect; and within and above all is the Divine Justice regulating the play of forces with the utmost mathematical accuracy, balancing cause and effect with the finest precision. But this Justice is not perceived—cannot be perceived—by those who are engaged in the conflict. Before this can be done, the fiercest warfare of passion must be left behind.

The world of passion is the abode of schisms, quarreling, wars, lawsuits, accusations, condemnations, impurities, weaknesses, follies, hatreds, revenges, and resentments. How can a man perceive Justice or understand Truth who is even partly involved in the fierce play of its blinding elements? As well expect a man caught in the flames of a burning building to sit down and reason out the cause of the fire.

In this realm of passion, men see injustice in the actions of others because, seeing only immediate appearances, they regard every act as standing by itself, undetached from cause and consequence. Having no knowledge of cause and effect in the moral sphere, people do not see the exacting and balancing process which is momentarily proceeding, nor do they regard their own actions as unjust, but only the actions of others.

A boy beats a defenseless animal, then a man beats the defenseless boy for his cruelty, then a stranger attacks the man for his cruelty to the boy. Each believes the other to be unjust and cruel, and himself to be just and humane; and doubtless most of all would the boy justify his conduct toward the animal as altogether necessary. Thus does ignorance keep alive hatred and strife. Thus do men blindly inflict suffering upon themselves, living in passion and resentment, and not finding the true way in life. Hatred is met by hatred, passion with passion, strife with strife. The man who kills is himself killed. The thief who lives by depriving others is himself deprived. The beast that preys on others is hunted and killed. The accuser is accused, the condemner is condemned, the denouncer is persecuted. Such is the Law.

Pain Is the Fruit of Passion

Passion, also, has its active and passive sides. Fool and fraud, oppressor and slave, aggressor and retaliator, the charlatan and the superstitious, complement each other, and come together by the operation of the Law of Justice. Men unconsciously cooperate in the mutual production of affliction; "the blind lead the blind, and both fall into the ditch." Pain, grief, sorrow, and misery are the fruits of which passion is the flower.

Where the passion-bound soul sees only injustice, the good man, he who has conquered passion, sees cause and effect, sees the Supreme Justice. It is impossible for such a man to regard himself as treated unjustly, because he has ceased to see injustice. He knows that no one can injure or cheat him, having ceased to injure or cheat himself. However passionately or ignorantly men may act towards him, it cannot possibly cause him any pain, for he knows that whatever comes to him (it may be abuse or persecution) can only come as an effect of what he himself has formerly sent out. He therefore regards all things as good, rejoices in all things, loves his enemies and blesses them that curse him, regarding them as the blind but beneficial instruments by which he is enabled to pay his moral debts to the Great Law.

Consequences Cannot Be Escaped

The good man, having put away all resentment, retaliation, self-seeking, and egotism, has arrived at a state of equilibrium, and has thereby become identified with the Eternal and Universal Equilibrium. Having lifted himself above the blind forces, he contemplates them with a calm penetrating insight, like the solitary dweller upon a mountain who looks down upon the conflict of the storms beneath his feet. For him, injustice has ceased, and he sees ignorance and suffering on the one hand, and enlightenment and bliss on the other. He sees that not only do the fool and the slave need his sympathy, but that the fraud and the oppressor are equally in need of it, and so his compassion is extended to all.

The Supreme Justice and the Supreme Love are one. Cause and effect cannot be avoided; consequences cannot be escaped.

While a man is given to hatred, resentment, anger, and condemnation, he is subject to injustice as the dreamer to his dream, and cannot do otherwise than see injustice. But he who has overcome those fiery and blinding elements knows that unerring Justice presides over all, that in reality there is no such thing as injustice in the whole of the universe.

The Use of Reason

WE HAVE HEARD IT SAID that reason is a blind guide, and that it draws men away from Truth rather than leads them to it. If this were true, it would be better to remain, or to become, unreasonable, and to persuade others to do so. We have found, however, that the diligent cultivation of the divine faculty of reason brings about calmness and mental poise, and enables one to meet cheerfully the problems and difficulties of life.

It is true there is a higher light than reason, even that of the Spirit of Truth itself, but without the aid of reason, Truth cannot be apprehended. They who refuse to light the lamp of reason will never, while they so refuse, perceive the Light of Truth, for the light of reason is a reflection of that Light.

Reason is a purely abstract quality, and comes midway between the animal and divine consciousness in men and women. It leads, if rightly employed, from the darkness of one to the Light of the other. It is true that reason may be enlisted in the service of the lower, self-seeking nature, but this is only a result of its partial and imperfect exercise. A fuller development of reason leads away from the selfish nature, and ultimately allies the soul with the highest, the divine.

Reason Leads One Away from Passion

The spiritual Percival who, searching for the Holy Grail of the Perfect Life, is again and again "left alone, and wearying in a land of sand and thorns" is not so stranded because he has followed reason, but because he is still reluctant to leave some remnants of his lower nature. He who will use the light of reason as a torch to search for Truth will not be left at last in comfortless darkness.

"Come, now, and let us reason together," saith the Lord, "though your sins be as scarlet, they shall be as white as snow."

Many men and women pass through untold sufferings, and at last die in their sins, because they refuse to reason. They cling to those dark delusions which even a faint glimmer of the light of reason would dispel. All must use their reason freely, fully, and faithfully, who would exchange the scarlet robe of sin and suffering for the white garment of blamelessness and peace.

It is because we have proved and know these truths that we exhort men to "tread the middle road, whose course bright reason traces, and soft quiet soothes." For reason leads away from passion and selfishness into the quiet ways of sweet persuasion and gentle forgiveness. He will never be led astray, nor will he follow blind guides, who faithfully adheres to the Apostolic injunction, "Prove all things, and hold fast that which is good." They, therefore, who despise the light of reason despise the Light of Truth.

Reason Is Concerned with Truth

Large numbers of people are possessed of the strange delusion that reason somehow is intimately connected with the denial of the existence of God. This is probably due to the fact that those who try to prove that there is no God usually profess to take their stand upon reason, while those who try to prove the reverse generally profess to take their stand on faith. Such argumentative combatants, however, are frequently governed more by prejudice than either reason or faith, their object being not to find Truth, but to defend and confirm a preconceived opinion.

Reason is concerned, not with ephemeral opinions, but with the established truth of things. He who is possessed of the faculty of reason in its purity and excellence can never be enslaved by prejudice, and will put from him all preconceived opinions as worthless. He will either attempt to prove or disprove, but after balancing extremes and bringing together all apparent contradictions, he will carefully and dispassionately weigh and consider them, and so arrive at Truth.

Reason is, in reality, associated with all that is pure and gentle, moderate and just. It is said of a violent man that he is "unreasonable," of a kind and considerate man that he is "reasonable," and of an insane man that he "has lost his reason." Thus it is seen that the word is used, even to a great extent unconsciously, though none the less truly, in a very comprehensive sense. And though reason is not actually love and thoughtfulness and gentleness and sanity, it leads to and is intimately connected with these divine qualities, and cannot, except for purposes of analysis, be dissociated from them.

Reason Almost Embraces Truth

Reason represents all that is high and noble in

man. It distinguishes him from the brute which blindly follows its animal inclinations, and just in the degree that man disobeys the voice of reason does he become brutish. As Milton says:

Reason in man obscured, or not obeyed
Immediately inordinate desires
And upstart passions catch the government
From reason, and to servitude reduce
Man till then free.

The following definition of "reason" from the dictionary will give some idea of the comprehensiveness of the word:

"The cause, ground, principle, or motive of anything said or done; efficient cause; final cause; the faculty of intelligence in man; especially the faculty by which we arrive at necessary truth."

It will thus be seen that "reason" is a term the breadth of which is almost sufficient to embrace even Truth itself, and Archbishop Trench tells us in his celebrated work "On the Study of Words" that the terms Reason and Word "are indeed so essentially one and the same that the Greek language has one word for both," so that the Word of God is the Reason of God. And one of the renderings of Lao-tze's "Tao" is Reason, so that in the Chinese translation of our New Testament, St. John's Gospel runs: "In the beginning was the Tao."

To the underdeveloped and uncharitable mind all words have narrow applications, but as a man enlarges his sympathies and broadens his intelligence, words become filled with rich meanings and assume comprehensive proportions. Let us therefore cease from foolish quarreling about words, and, like reasonable beings, search for principles, and practice those things which make for unity and peace.

Self-Discipline

A MAN DOES NOT LIVE until he begins to discipline himself; he merely exists. Like an animal he gratifies his desires and pursues his inclinations just where they may lead him. He is happy as a beast is happy, because he is not conscious of what he is depriving himself. He suffers as the beast suffers, because he does not know the way out of suffering. He does not intelligently reflect upon life, and lives a series of sensations, longings, and confused memories which are unrelated to any central idea or principle.

A man whose inner life is so ungoverned and chaotic must necessarily manifest this confusion in the visible conditions of his outer life in the world. And though for a time, running with the stream of his desires, he may draw to himself a more or less large share of the outer necessities and comforts of life, he never achieves any real success nor accomplishes any real good. Sooner or later worldly failure and disaster are inevitable, as the direct outcome of the inward failure to properly adjust and regulate those mental forces which make the outer life.

Before a man can accomplish anything of enduring nature in the world, he must first of all acquire some measure of success in the management of his own mind. This is as mathematical a truism as that two and two are four, for "out of the heart are the issues of life." If a man cannot govern the forces within himself, he cannot long hold a firm hand upon the outer activities which form his visible life. On the other hand, as a man succeeds in governing himself he rises to higher and higher levels of power and usefulness and success in the world.

Practicing Self-Discipline

The only difference between the life of the beast and that of the undisciplined man is that the man has a wider variety of desires, and experiences a greater intensity of suffering. It may be said of such a man that he is dead, being truly dead to self-control, chastity, fortitude, and all the nobler qualities which constitute life. In the consciousness of such a man the crucified Christ lies entombed, awaiting that resurrection which shall revitalize the mortal sufferer, and wake him up to a knowledge of the realities of his existence.

With the practice of self-discipline a man begins to live, for then he commences to rise above the inward confusion and to adjust his conduct to a steadfast center within himself. He ceases to follow where inclination leads him, reins in the steed of his desires, and lives in accordance with the dictates of reason and wisdom. Before his life has been without purpose or meaning, but now he begins to consciously mold his own destiny. He is "clothed and in his right mind."

Control—The First Stage of Self-Discipline

In the process of self-discipline there are three stages, namely:

1. Control
2. Purification
3. Relinquishment

A man begins to discipline himself by controlling those passions which have hitherto controlled him. He resists temptation, and guards himself against all those tendencies to selfish gratification which are so easy and natural, and which have formerly dominated him. He brings his appetite into subjection, and begins to eat as a reasonable and responsible being. He practices moderation and thoughtfulness in the selection of food, with the object of making his body a pure instrument through which he may live and act as becomes a man, and no longer degrading that body by pandering to gustatory pleasure. He puts a check upon his tongue, his temper, and, in fact, his every animal desire and tendency, and this he does by referring all his acts to a fixed center within himself.

It is a process of living from within outward, instead of, as formerly, from without inward. He conceives of an ideal, and, enshrining that ideal in the sacred recesses of his heart, he regulates his conduct in accordance with its exactions and demands.

There is a philosophical hypothesis that at the heart of every atom and every aggregation of atoms in the universe there is a motionless center which is the sustaining source of all the universal activities. Be this as it may, there is certainly in the heart of every man and woman a selfless center without which the outer man could not be, and the ignoring of which leads to suffering and confusion. This selfless center which takes the form, in the mind, of an ideal of unselfishness and spotless purity, the attainment of which is desirable, is man's eternal refuge from the storms of passion and all the conflicting elements of his lower nature. It is the Rock of Ages, the Christ within, the divine and immortal in all men.

As a man practices self-control, he approximates more and more to this inward reality, and is less and less swayed by passion and grief, pleasure and pain. He lives a steadfast and virtuous life, manifesting strength and fortitude. The restraining of the passions, however, is merely the initial stage in self-discipline, and is immediately followed by the process of Purification. By this a man so purifies himself as to take passion out of the heart and mind altogether; not merely restraining it when it rises within him, but preventing it from rising altogether. By merely restraining his passions, a man can never arrive at peace, can never actualize his ideal. He must purify those passions.

Purification—The Second Stage of Self-Discipline

It is in the purification of his lower nature that a man becomes strong and god-like, standing firmly upon the ideal center within, and rendering all temptations powerless and ineffectual. This purification is effected by thoughtful care, earnest meditation, and holy aspiration. As success is achieved, confusion of mind and life pass away, and calmness of mind and spiritualized conduct ensue.

True strength and power and usefulness are born of self-purification, for the lower animal forces are not lost, but are transmuted into intellectual and spiritual energy. The pure life (pure in thought and deed) is a life of conservation of energy. The impure life (even should the impurity not extend beyond thought) is a life of dissipation of energy. The pure man is more capable, and therefore more fit to succeed in his plans and to accomplish his purposes than the impure. Where the impure man fails, the pure man will step up and be victorious, because he directs his energies with a calmer mind and greater definiteness and strength of purpose.

With the growth of purity, all the elements which constitute a strong and virtuous manhood are developed in an increasing degree of power. As a man brings his lower nature into subjection, and makes his passions do his bidding, just so much will he mold the outer circumstances of his life, and influence others for good.

Relinquishment—The Third Stage of Self-Discipline

The third stage of self-discipline, that of Relinquishment, is a process of letting the lower desires and all impure and unworthy thoughts drop out of the mind, and refusing to give them any admittance, leaving them to perish. As a man grows purer, he perceives that all evil is powerless, unless it receives his encouragement, and so he ignores it, and lets it pass out of his life.

It is pursuing this aspect of self-discipline that a man enters into and realizes the divine life. He manifests those qualities which are distinctly divine, such as wisdom, patience, non-resistance, compassion, and love. It is here, also, where a man becomes consciously immortal, rising above all the fluctuations and uncertainties of life, and living in an intelligent and unchangeable peace.

By self-discipline a man attains to every degree of virtue and holiness, and finally becomes a purified son of God, realizing his oneness with the central heart of all things.

Without self-discipline a man drifts lower and lower, approximating more and more nearly to the beast, until at last he grovels, a lost creature, in the mire of his own befoulment. By self-discipline a man rises higher and higher, approximating more and more nearly to the divine, until at last he stands erect in his divine dignity, a saved soul, glorified by the radiance of his purity. Let a man discipline himself, and he will live; let a man cease to discipline himself, and he will perish. As a tree grows in beauty, health, and fruitfulness by being carefully pruned and tended, so a man grows in grace and beauty of life by cutting away the branches of evil from his mind. And as he tends, he develops the good by constant and unfailing effort.

As a man by practice acquires proficiency in his craft, so the earnest man acquires proficiency in goodness and wisdom. Men shrink from self-discipline because in its early stages it is painful and repellent, and the yielding to desire is, at first, sweet and inviting. But the end of desire is darkness and unrest, whereas the fruits of discipline are immortality and peace.

Resolution

RESOLUTION IS THE DIRECTING and impelling force in individual progress. Without it no substantial work can be accomplished. Not until a man brings resolution to bear upon his life does he consciously and rapidly develop, for a life without resolution is a life without aims. And a life without aims is a drifting and unstable thing.

Resolution may, of course, be linked to downward tendencies, but it is more usually the companion of noble aims and lofty ideals, and I am dealing with it in this, its highest use and application.

When a man makes a resolution, it means that he is dissatisfied with his condition. He is commencing to take himself in hand with a view to producing a better piece of workmanship out of the mental materials of which his character and life are composed. And insofar as he is true to his resolution, he will succeed in accomplishing his purpose.

The vows of the saintly ones are holy resolutions

directed toward some victory over self, and the beautiful achievements of holy ones and the glorious conquests of the Divine Teachers were rendered possible and actual by the pursuit of unswerving resolution.

To arrive at the fixed determination to walk a higher path than before, although it reveals the great difficulties which have to be surmounted, it yet makes possible the treading of that path, and illuminates its dark places with the golden halo of success.

Be Slow to Make Resolutions

The true resolution is the crisis of long thought, protracted struggle, or fervent but unsatisfied aspiration. It is no light thing, no whimsical impulse or vague desire, but a solemn and irrevocable determination not to rest or cease from effort until the high purpose, which is held in view, is fully accomplished.

Half-hearted and premature resolution is no resolution at all, and is shattered at the first difficulty.

A man should be slow to form a resolution. He should searchingly examine his position and take into consideration every circumstance and difficulty connected with his decision, and should be fully prepared to meet them. He should be sure that he completely understands the nature of his resolution, that his mind is finally made up, and that he is without fear and doubt in the matter. With the mind thus prepared, the resolution that is formed will not be diluted, and by the aid of it a man will, in due time, accomplish his strong purpose.

Hasty resolutions are futile. The mind must be fortified to endure.

A soon as the resolution to walk a higher path is made, temptation and trial begin. Men have found that no sooner have they decided to lead a truer and nobler life than they have been overwhelmed with such a torrent of new temptations and difficulties as to make their position almost unendurable. And many men, because of this, relinquish their resolution.

But these temptations and trials are a necessary part of the work of regeneration upon which the man has decided. They must be hailed as friends and met with courage if the resolution is to work.

Cutting a New Channel

What is the nature of a resolution? Is it not the sudden checking of a particular stream of conduct, and the endeavor to open up an entirely new channel? Think of an engineer who decides to turn the course of a powerfully running stream or river in another direction. He must first cut his new channel, and must take every precaution to avoid failure in the carrying out of his undertaking. But when he comes to the all-important task of directing the stream into its new channel, then the flowing force, which for ages has steadily pursued its accustomed course, becomes unmanageable, and all the patience, care, and skill of the engineer will be required for the successful completion of the work. It is even so with the man who determines to turn his course of conduct in another and higher direction.

Having prepared his mind, which is the cutting of a new channel, he then proceeds to the work of redirecting his mental forces—which have hitherto flowed on uninterruptedly—into the new course. As soon as this is attempted, the arrested energy begins to assert itself into the form of powerful temptations and trials hitherto unknown and unencountered. And this is exactly as it should be. It is the law; and the same law that is in the water is in the mind.

No man can improve upon the established law of things, but he can learn to understand the law instead of complaining and wishing things were different. The man who understands all that is involved in the regeneration of his mind will "glory in tribulations," knowing that only by passing through them can he gain strength, obtain purity of heart, and arrive at peace. And as the engineer at last (perhaps after many mistakes and failures) succeeds in getting the stream to flow peacefully in the broader and better channel, and the turbulence of the water is spent, and all dams can be removed, so the man of resolution at last succeeds in directing his thoughts and acts into the better and nobler way to which he aspires, and temptations and trials give way to steadfast strength and settled peace.

Be True to Your Decision

He whose life is not in harmony with his conscience, and who is anxious to remedy his mind and conduct in a particular direction, let him first mature his purpose by earnest thought and self-examination. Having arrived at a final conclusion, let him frame his resolution, and having done so let him not swerve from it. Let him remain true to his decision under all circumstances, and he cannot fail to achieve his good purpose. For the Great Law ever shields and protects him who, no matter how deep his sins, or how great and many his failures and mistakes, has, deep in his heart resolved upon the finding of a better way. Then every obstacle must at last give way before a matured and unshaken resolution.

The Glorious Conquest

Truth can only be apprehended by the conquest of self. Blessedness can only be arrived at by overcoming the lower nature. The water of Truth is barred by a man's self. The only enemies that can actually hinder him are his own passions and delusions. Until a man realizes this and commences to cleanse his heart, he has not found the Path which leads to knowledge and peace. Until passion is transcended, Truth remains unknown. This is the Divine Law.

A man cannot keep his passions and have Truth as well. Error is not slain until selfishness is dead. The overcoming of self is no mystical theory, but a very real and practical thing. It is a process which must be pursued daily and hourly, with unswerving faith and undaunted resolution if any measure of success is to be achieved.

The process is one of orderly growth, having its

sequential stages, like the growth of a tree. As fruit can only be produced by carefully and patiently training the tree, even so the pure and satisfying fruits of holiness can only be obtained by faithfully and patiently training the mind in the growth of right thought and conduct.

The Five Steps

There are five steps in the overcoming of passion (which includes all bad habits and particular forms of wrongdoing), which I call:

1. Repression
2. Endurance
3. Elimination
4. Understanding
5. Victory.

When men fail to overcome their passions, it is because they try to begin at the wrong end. They want to have the stage of Victory without passing through the previous four stages. They are in the position of the gardener who wants to produce good fruit without training and attending to his trees.

Step One: *Repression*

Repression consists in checking and controlling the wrong act (such as an outburst of temper, a hasty or unkind word, a selfish indulgence, etc.), and not allowing it to take actual form. This is equivalent to the gardener's nipping off the useless buds and branches from the tree. It is a necessary process, and painful. The tree bleeds while undergoing the process and the gardener knows that it must not be taxed too severely. The heart also bleeds when it refuses to return passion for passion, when it ceases to defend and justify itself. It is the process of "mortifying the members" of which St. Paul speaks.

But this repression is only the beginning of self-conquest. When it is made an end in itself, and there is no goal of finally purifying the heart, that is a stage of hypocrisy; a hiding of one's true nature, and striving to appear better in the eyes of others than one really is. In that case it is evil, but when adopted as the first stage toward complete purification, it is good.

Step Two: *Endurance*

The practice of repression leads to the second stage *Endurance*, or forbearance, in which one silently endures the pain which arises in the mind when it is brought in contact with certain actions and attitudes of other minds. As success is attained in this stage, the striver comes to see that all his pain actually arises in his own weakness, and not in the wrong attitudes of others toward him, these latter being merely the means by which his passions are brought to the surface and revealed to him. He thus gradually exonerates all others from blame in his falls and lapses of conduct. He accuses only himself, and so learns to love those who unconsciously reveal to him his passions and shortcomings.

Step Three: *Elimination*

Having passed through these two stages of self-crucifixion (repression and endurance), the disciple enters the third, that of *Elimination*, in which all wrong is cast from the mind immediately as it appears. At this stage, conscious strength and holy joy begin to take the place of pain. With the mind having become comparatively calm, the striver is enabled to gain a deeper insight into the complexities of his mind, and thus to understand the inception, growth, and outworking of passion. This leads to the stage of *Understanding*.

Step Four: ***Understanding***

Perfection in *Understanding* leads to the final conquest of self, a conquest so complete that passion can no longer arise in the mind even as a thought or impression. For when knowledge of passion is complete, when it is known in its totality, from its inception as a seed in the mind to its ripened outgrowth as act and consequence, then it can no more be allowed a place in life, but is abandoned forever. Then the mind is at peace. The wrong acts of others no longer arouse wrong and pain in the mind of the disciple. He or she is glad and calm and wise. He or she is filled with Love, and blessedness abides within.

Step Five: And this is ***Victory!***

Contentment in Activity

THE CONFOUNDING of a positive spiritual virtue or principle with a negative animal vice is common among writers even of what is called the "Advanced School of Thought." Much valuable energy is frequently expended in criticizing and condemning, where a little calm reasoning would have revealed a greater light, and have led to the exercise of a broader charity.

The other day I came across a vigorous attack upon the teachings of "Love" wherein the writer condemned the teaching as weakly, foolish, and hypocritical. Needless to say, that which he was condemning as "Love" was merely weak sentimentality and hypocrisy.

Another writer in condemning "meekness" does not know that what he calls meekness is only cowardice; while another who attacks "chastity" as "a snare" is really confusing painful and hypocritical restraint with the virtue of chastity. And just lately I received a long letter from a correspondent who took great pains to show me that "contentment" is a vice, and is the source of innumerable evils.

That which my correspondent called "contentment" is, of course, animal indifference. The spirit of indifference is incompatible with progress, whereas the spirit of contentment may, and does, attend the highest form of activity, the truest advancement and development. Indolence is the twin sister of indifference, but cheerful and ready action is the friend of contentment.

Contentment Is Abiding Joy

Contentment is a virtue which becomes lofty and spiritual in its later development, as the mind is trained to perceive and the heart to receive the guidance, in all things, of a merciful law.

To be contented does not mean to forgo effort; it means to free effort from anxiety. It does not mean to be satisfied with sin, ignorance, and folly, but to rest happily in duty done and work accomplished.

A man may be said to be content to lead a groveling life, to remain in sin and in debt, but such a man's true state is one of indifference to his duty, obligations, and the just claims of others. He cannot truly be said to possess the virtue of contentment. He does not experience the pure and abiding joy which is the accompaniment of active contentment. And, so far as his true nature is concerned, he is a sleeping soul, who, sooner or later, will be awakened by intense suffering, which having passed through, he will find that true contentment which is the outcome of honest effort and true living.

There are three things with which a man should be content:

1. With whatever happens
2. With his friendships and possessions
3. With his pure thoughts.

Contented with whatever happens, he will escape grief. With friends and possessions, he will avoid anxiety and wretchedness; and with pure thoughts, he will never go back to suffer and grovel in impurities.

There are three things with which a man should not be content:

1. With his opinions
2. With his character
3. With his spiritual condition.

Not content with his opinions, he will continually increase in intelligence. Not content with his character, he will ceaselessly grow in strength and virtue; and not content with his spiritual condition, he will, every day, enter into a larger wisdom and fuller blessedness. In a word, a man should be contented, but not indifferent to his development as a responsible spiritual being.

The truly contented man works energetically and faithfully, and accepts all results with an untroubled spirit, trusting, at first, that all is well. Afterwards, with the growth of enlightenment, he knows that results exactly correspond with efforts. Whatsoever material possessions that come, come not by greed and anxiety and strife, but by right action, wise action, and pure exertion.

The Temple of Brotherhood

UNIVERSAL BROTHERHOOD is the Supreme Ideal of Humanity, and towards that Ideal the world is slowly but surely moving. Today, as never before, numbers of earnest men and women are striving to make this Ideal tangible and real. Fraternities are springing up on every land, and press and pulpit, the world over, are preaching the Brotherhood of Man.

The unselfish elements in all such efforts cannot fail to have their effect upon the race, and are with certainty urging it towards the goal of its noblest inspirations. But the ideal state has not yet manifested through any outward organization, and societies formed for the purpose of propagating Brotherhood are continually being shattered to pieces by inner dissension.

The Brotherhood for which humanity sighs is

withheld from actuality by humanity itself; nay, more, it is frustrated even by men who work zealously for it as a desirable possibility. This is because the purely spiritual nature of Brotherhood is not perceived, and the principles involved, as well as the individual course of conduct necessary to perfect unity, are not comprehended.

Brotherhood, as a human organization, cannot exist so long as any degree of self-seeking reigns in the hearts of men and women who band themselves together for any purpose, as such self-seeking must eventually tear the seamless coat of loving unity. But although organized Brotherhood has so far largely failed, any person may realize Brotherhood in its perfection, and know it in all its beauty and completion, if he will make himself a wise, pure, loving spirit. He must remove from his mind every element of strife, and learn to practice those divine qualities without which Brotherhood is but a mere theory, opinion, or elusive dream.

For Brotherhood is at first spiritual, and its outer manifestation in the world must follow as a natural sequence.

As a spiritual reality it must be discovered by each man for himself, and in the only place where spiritual realities can be found—within himself, and it rests with each whether he shall choose or refuse it.

The Four Enemies of Brotherhood

There are four chief tendencies in the human mind which are destructive of Brotherhood, and which bar the way to its comprehension, namely:

1. Pride
2. Self-love
3. Hatred
4. Condemnation.

Where these are, there can be no Brotherhood. In whatsoever heart these hold sway, discord rules, and Brotherhood is not realized, for these tendencies are, in their very nature, dark and selfish, and always make for disruption and destruction. From these four things proceeds that serpent brood of false actions and conditions which poison the heart, and fill the world with suffering and sorrow.

Out of the spirit of pride proceed envy, resentment, and attachment to opinion. Pride envies the position, influence, or goodness of others. Pride thinks, "I am more deserving than this man or this woman." It also continually finds occasion for resenting the actions of others, and says, "I have been snubbed; I have been insulted," and, thinking altogether of its own excellence, it sees no excellence in others.

From the spirit of self-love proceed egotism, lust for power, disparagement and contempt. Self-love worships the personality in which it moves. It is lost in the adoration and glorification of that "I," that "self" which has no real existence, but is a dark dream and delusion. It desires preeminence over others, and thinks, "I am great," "I am more important than others." It also disparages others and bestows upon them contempt, seeing no beauty in them, being lost in the contemplation of its own beauty.

From the spirit of hatred proceed slander, cruelty, criticism, and anger. It strives to overcome evil by adding evil to it. It says, "This man has spoken ill of me, I will speak more ill of him and thus teach him a lesson." It mistakes cruelty for kindness, and causes its possessor to revile a reproving friend. It feeds the flame of anger with bitter and rebellious thoughts.

From the spirit of condemnation proceed accusation, false pity, and false judgment. It feeds itself on the contemplation of evil, and cannot see the good. It has eyes for evil only, and finds it in almost every thing and every person. It sets up an arbitrary standard of right and wrong by which to judge others, and it thinks, "This man does not do as I would have him do; he is therefore evil, and I will denounce him." So blind is the spirit of condemnation that while rendering its possessor incapable of judging himself, it causes him to set himself up as the judge of all the earth.

From the four tendencies enumerated, no element of brotherliness can proceed. They are deadly mental poisons, and anyone who allows them to rankle the mind cannot apprehend the peaceful principles on which Brotherhood rests.

The Four Divine Qualities

Then there are chiefly four divine qualities which are productive of Brotherhood; which are, as it were, the foundation-stones on which it rests, namely:

1. Humility
2. Self-surrender
3. Love
4. Compassion.

Wheresoever these are, there Brotherhood is

active. In whatsoever heart these qualities are dominant, there Brotherhood is an established reality, for they are, in their very nature, unselfish, and are revealed with the revealing Light of Truth. There is no darkness in them, and where they are, so powerful is their light, that the dark tendencies cannot remain, but are dissolved and dissipated.

Out of these four qualities proceed all those angelic actions and conditions which make for unity and bring gladness to the heart of man and the world.

From the spirit of Humility proceed meekness and peacefulness; from Self-surrender come patience, wisdom and true judgment; from Love spring kindness, joy, and harmony; and from Compassion proceed gentleness and forgiveness.

He who has brought himself into harmony with these four qualities is divinely enlightened. He sees whence the actions of man proceed and whither they tend, and therefore can no longer live in the exercise of the dark tendencies. He has realized Brotherhood in its completion as freedom from malice, from envy, from bitterness, from contention, from condemnation. All men are his brothers, those who live in the dark tendencies, as well as those who live in the enlightening qualities, for he knows that when they have perceived the glory and the beauty of the Light of the Truth, the dark tendencies will be dispelled from their minds. He has but one attitude of mind towards all, that of good-will.

Of the four dark tendencies are born ill-will and strife; of the four divine qualities are born good-will and peace.

Living in the four tendencies, a man is a strife-producer. Living in the four qualities, a man is a peacemaker.

Involved in the darkness of the selfish tendencies, men believe that they can fight for peace, kill to make alive, slay injury by injuring, restore love by hatred, unity by contention, kindness by cruelty, and establish Brotherhood by erecting their own opinions (which they themselves will, in the course of time, abandon as worthless) as objects of universal adoration.

The wished-for Temple of Brotherhood will be erected in the world when its four foundation-stones of Humility, Self-surrender, Love and Compassion are firmly laid in the hearts of men, for Brotherhood consists, first of all, in the abandonment of self by the individual, and its aftereffect is unity between man and man.

One Must Practice Brotherhood

Theories and schemes for propagating Brotherhood are many, but Brotherhood itself is one and unchangeable. It consists in the complete cessation from egotism and strife, and in practicing good-will and peace; for Brotherhood is a practice and not a theory. Self-surrender and Good-will are its guardian angels, and peace is its habitation.

When two are determined to maintain an opposing opinion, the clinging to self and ill-will are there, and Brotherhood is absent.

When two are prepared to sympathize with each other, to see no evil in each other, to serve and not to attack each other, the love of Truth and Good-will are there, and Brotherhood is present.

All strife, divisions, and wars inhere in the proud, unyielding self. All peace, unity, and friendship inhere in the Principles which the yielding up of self reveals.

Brotherhood is only practiced and known by one whose heart is at peace with all the world.

Pleasant Pastures of Peace

HE WHO ASPIRES to the bettering of himself and humanity should ceaselessly strive to arrive at the exercise of that blessed attitude of mind by which he is enabled to put himself mentally and sympathetically in the place of others. Instead of harshly and falsely judging them, and thereby making himself unhappy without adding to the happiness of those others, he will enter into their experience, will understand their particular frame of mind, and will feel for them and sympathize with them.

One of the great obstacles to the attainment of such an attitude of mind is prejudice, and until this is removed it is impossible to act toward others as we would wish others to act toward us.

Prejudice is destructive of kindness, sympathy, love, and true judgment, and the strength of a man's prejudice will be the measure of his harshness and unkindness toward others, for prejudice and cruelty are inseparable.

There is no rationality in prejudice. As soon as it is aroused in a man he ceases to act as a reasonable being, and gives way to rashness, anger, and injurious excitement. He does not consider his words nor regard the feelings and liberties of those at whom his prejudices are directed. He has, for the time being, forfeited his manhood, and has descended to the level of an irrational creature.

While a man is determined to cling to his preconceived opinions, mistaking them for Truth, and refuses to consider dispassionately the position of others, he cannot escape hatred nor arrive at blessedness.

The man who strives after gentleness, who aspires to act unselfishly toward others, will put away all his passionate prejudices and petty opinions. He will gradually acquire the power of thinking and feeling for others, of understanding their particular state of ignorance or knowledge, and thereby enter fully into their hearts and lives, sympathizing with them, and seeing them as they are.

Such a man will not oppose himself to the prejudices of others by introducing his own way, but will seek to diminish prejudice by introducing sympathy and love, striving to bring out all that is good in men, encouraging the good by appealing to it, and discouraging the evil by ignoring it. He will realize the good in the unselfish efforts of others, though their outward methods may be different from his own, and will so rid his heart of hatred, and will fill it with love and blessedness.

Evil Is Only Overcome by Good

When a man is prone to harshly judge and condemn others, he should inquire how far he falls short himself. He should also reconsider those periods of suffering when he himself was misjudged and misunderstood. Gathering wisdom and love from his own bitter experience, he should studiously and self-sacrificingly refrain from piercing with anguish hearts that are as yet too weak to ignore, too immature and uninstructed to understand.

Sympathy is not required towards those who are purer and more enlightened than one's self, as the purer one lives above the necessity for it. In such a case, reverence should be exercised, with a striving to lift one's self up to the purer level, and so enter into possession of the larger life. Nor can a man fully understand one who is wiser than himself. Before condemning, he should earnestly ask himself whether he is, after all, better than the man whom he has singled out as the object of his bitterness. If he is, let him bestow sympathy. If he is not, let him exercise reverence.

For thousands of years the sages have taught, both by precept and example, that evil is only overcome by good, yet still that lesson, for the majority, remains unlearned. It is a lesson profound in its simplicity, and difficult to learn because men are blinded by the illusions of self. Men are still engaged in resenting, condemning, and fighting the evil in their fellow-men, thereby increasing the delusion in their own hearts, and adding to the world's sum of misery and suffering. When they find out that their own resentment must be eradicated, and love put in its place, evil will perish for lack of sustenance.

With burning brain and heart of hate,
I sought my wronger, early, late,
And all the wretched night and day
My dream and thought was slay, and slay.
My better self rose uppermost,

The beast within my bosom lost
Itself in love; peace from afar
Shone o'er me radiant like a star.
I slew my wronger with a deed,
A deed of love; I made him bleed
With kindness, and I filled for years
His soul with tenderness and tears.

Dislike, resentment, and condemnation are all forms of hatred, and evil cannot cease until these are taken out of the heart.

But the obliterating of injuries from the mind is merely one of the beginnings in wisdom. There is a still higher and better way. And that way is to so purify the heart and enlighten the mind that, far from having to forget injuries, there will be none to remember. For it is only pride and self that can be injured and wounded by the actions and attitudes of others. He who takes pride and self out of the heart can never think the thought, "I have been injured by another," or "I have been wronged by another."

Purge Evil from Your Heart

From a purified heart proceeds the right comprehension of things; and from the right comprehension of things proceeds the life that is peaceful, freed from bitterness and suffering, calm and wise. He who thinks, "This man has injured me," has not perceived the Truth in life. He falls short of that enlightenment which disperses the erroneous idea of evil as a thing to be hatefully resented. He who is troubled and disturbed about the sins of others is far from the Truth; he who is troubled and disturbed about his own sins is very near to the Gate of Wisdom. He in whose heart the flames of resentment burn cannot know Peace nor understand Truth. He who will banish resentment from his heart will know and understand.

He who has taken evil out of his own heart cannot resent or resist it in others, for he is enlightened as to its origin and nature, and knows it as a manifestation of the mistakes of ignorance. With the increase of enlightenment, sin becomes impossible. He who sins does not understand; he who understands does not sin.

The pure man maintains his tenderness of heart toward those who ignorantly imagine they can do him harm. The wrong attitude of others toward him does not trouble him; his heart is at rest in Compassion and Love.

Blessed is he who has no wrongs to remember, no

injuries to forget; in whose pure heart no hateful thought about another can take root and flourish.

Let those who aim at the right life, who believe that they love Truth, cease to passionately oppose themselves to others. Let them strive to calmly and wisely understand them, and in thus acting toward others they will be conquering themselves. While sympathizing with others, their own souls will be fed with the heavenly dew of kindness, and their hearts will be strengthened and refreshed in the pleasant Pastures of Peace.

Book Three

The Life Triumphant

Hail to Thee, Man divine! the conqueror
Of sin and shame and sorrow; no more weak,
Wormlike, and groveling art thou; no, nor
Wilt thou again bow down to things that wreak
Scourgings and death upon thee; thou dost rise
Triumphant in thy strength; good, pure and wise.

The Life Triumphant

Table of Contents

Foreword

EVERY BEING LIVES in his own mental world. His joys and sorrows are the creations of his own mind, and are dependent upon the mind for their existence. In the midst of the world, darkened with many sins and sorrows, in which the majority live, there abides another world, lighted up with shining virtues and unpolluted joy, in which the perfect ones live. This world can be found and entered, and the way to it is by self-control and moral excellence. It is the world of the perfect life, and it rightly belongs to man, who is not complete until crowned with perfection. The perfect life is not the faraway, impossible thing that men who are in darkness imagine it to be; it is supremely possible, and very near and real. Man remains a craving, weeping, sinning, repenting creature just so long as he wills to do so by clinging to those weak conditions. But when he wills to shake off his dark dreams and to rise, he arises and achieves.

—James Allen

Faith and Courage

FOR THOSE WHO WILL FIGHT BRAVELY and not yield, there is triumphant victory over all the dark things of life. I state this at the beginning, that the reader may know there is no uncertainty about it. In the course of this book I shall show what are the elements, in character and conduct, which go to build up the life of calm strength and superlative victory.

To stand face to face with truth; to arrive, after innumerable wanderings and pains, at wisdom and bliss; not to be finally defeated and cast out, but ultimately to triumph over every inward foe—such is man's divine destiny, such his glorious goal. And this, every saint, sage, and savior has declared.

The School of Life

In the present stage of the life of humanity, comparatively few reach this place of triumph—though all will reach it at last—yet there is a glorious company of perfect ones who have attained in the past, and their number is being added to with each succeeding age. Men are as yet learners in the school of life, and most men die learners. But there are some who, in this life, through fixity of purpose and strenuous fighting against darkness, pain, and ignorance, acquire a right knowledge of life and pass joyfully beyond the pupil stage.

Man is not to remain forever a schoolboy in the universe, to be whipped for follies and errors. When he wills and wishes, he can set his mind upon his task and master the lessons of life, becoming a confident and skilled scholar, living in understanding and peace, and not in ignorance and misery.

The sorrows of life are profound and deeply rooted, but they can be fathomed and rooted out. The passions and emotions of human nature are, in their ungoverned state, overwhelming and painfully conflicting, but they can be so softened down, harmonized, and wisely directed and understood, as to become obedient servants for the outworking of enlightened purposes.

The difficulties of life are great, its battle fierce, and its wished-for issues are uncertain and elusive;

so much so, that every hour men and women are breaking down under the strain. Yet these conditions have no objective and arbitrary existence. In their true nature they are subjective and purely mental, and can be transcended. There is no inherent and permanent evil in the universal order; and the mind can be lifted up to the moral altitude where evil can touch it no more.

Faith Precedes Knowledge

A steadfast faith in an Eternal and Universal Justice, in an over-ruling Good, is the prelude to the Life Triumphant. The man who aims to become strong, serene, and steadfast at heart must, at the onset, have no doubt that the Heart of Life is good. He who is to gaze upon the Cosmic Order and experience the rapture of emancipation must realize that there is no disorder in his life but that which he creates. This realization is difficult, so prone is the mind, in its imperfect stages, to self-pity and self-justification, but it can be attained, and must be attained by him who is to live the freed life. At first it must be believed, and the belief must be adhered to, until it ripens into realization and knowledge.

The sufferings of life are greatly reduced when

they are accepted as disciplinary experiences, and the man of faith does so accept them. The sufferings of life are transcended and put away when all experiences are accounted good, and are utilized in the development of character, and the man of knowledge does so regard and utilize them.

Faith is the grey dawn which precedes the full and perfect day of knowledge. Without it there can be no attainment of strength, no permanent security of heart. The man of faith does not succumb when difficulties present themselves; he does not despair when troubles overtake him. However steep and dark his path may seem, he looks forward to a brighter pathway ahead. He sees a destination of rest and light beyond.

They who have no faith in the triumph of good ignominiously succumb to the elements of evil. And this must be so; for he who does not elevate good, elevates evil, and, seeing evil as the master of life, he receives the wages of evil.

Evil is Blind to Its Folly

There are those who, having yielded to defeat in the battle of life, talk thoughtlessly about the wrongs they have suffered at the hands of others. They believe—and try to make others believe—that they would have been successful or rich or famous but for the treachery and villainy of those about them. They tell, for the thousandth time, how they have been deceived, defrauded, and degraded by others. They imagine that they themselves are all trust, all innocence, all honesty and good nature, and that nearly everyone else is all that is bad and malicious. They tell how they would have been just as prosperous and honored as others if they had been as selfish as those others; and that their great drawback, and the chief source, in themselves, of their failures, is that they were born with too great an endowment of unselfishness.

Such self-praising complainers cannot distinguish between good and evil, and their faith in human nature and the goodness of the universe is dead. Looking upon others, they have eyes for evil only; looking upon themselves, they see only suffering innocence. Rather than discover any evil in themselves, they would have all humanity bad. In their hearts they have enthroned the wretched Demon of Evil as the Lord of Life, and see in the course of things only a selfish scramble in which the good is always crushed and the evil rises triumphant. Blind to their own folly, ignorance, and weakness, they see nothing but injustice in their fate, nothing but misery and wretchedness in their present condition.

Evil is Not More Powerful Than Good

He who would have even a useful and successful life—yet alone a spiritually noble and victorious one—must at once root out and cast away this wretched condition of mind that negates all that is good and pure, and gives preeminence to all that is base and impure. Misfortune, misery and defeat most surely await the man who believes that dishonesty, deceit and selfishness are the best weapons whereby to achieve a successful life. What courage and strength can a man develop, and what quiet and happiness can he enjoy, who believes that in order to keep pace with others he must continually deny and discourage the better qualities of his nature? The man who believes that evil is more powerful than good, and that bad men have the best of life, is still involved in the elements of evil; and, being so involved, he suffers—must necessarily suffer—defeat.

It may appear to you that the world is given over to wickedness; that the bad prosper, and the good fail; that there is nothing but chance, injustice, and disorder. But do not believe this: regard it as an illusive appearance. Conclude that you do not see life as it really is; that you have not yet fathomed the causes of things, and that when you can look upon life through a purer heart and a wiser mind, you will see and understand its equity. And truly when you do so look at life, you will see good where you now see evil, order where now appears disorder, and justice where now injustice seems to prevail.

The universe is a cosmos, not a chaos, and the bad do not prosper. It is true there is much evil in the world, otherwise there would be no necessity for moral aims, but there is also much misery in the world, and the evil and misery are related as cause and effect. It is equally true that there is much good in the world, and much abiding gladness, and the good and gladness are related as cause and effect.

He who has acquired that faith in the power and supremacy of good, which no apparent injustice, no amount of suffering, and no catastrophe can shake, will pass through all emergencies, all trials and difficulties, with a sublime courage that defies the demons of doubt and despair. He may not succeed in all his plans. He may even encounter much failure; but when he fails, it will be that he may frame nobler purposes and ascend to higher achievements. He will only fail in order to reach a success greater than that of which he first dreamed. His life will not, cannot, be a failure.

Some of its details will fail, but this will be but the breaking of weak links in the chain of character and events, in order that the whole may be made more strong and complete.

Faith is Not Theological Belief

There is an animal courage which can calmly face the fire of an enemy in battle, or the fierce rage of beasts, but which fails in the battle of life and breaks down when confronted with the beasts that rage within one's own heart. It requires a higher, diviner courage to remain calm in the hour of deprivation and calamity than in the heat of battle, to overcome self than to overcome another. And this diviner courage is the companion of faith.

A mere theological belief (commonly confused with faith) will not avail. Beliefs about God, Jesus, Creation, etc., are merely surface opinions (derived chiefly from custom) which do not reach down to the real life of a man and have no power to bestow faith. Such beliefs may accompany faith, but they are distinct from it. Frequently, those who hold most tenaciously to particular beliefs about God, Jesus, and the Bible are most lacking in faith—that is, they give way to complaint, despondency, and grief immediately after some petty trouble overtakes them. If one is given to irritability, anxiety, hopelessness, and lamentations over the simple things of life, let him know that, in spite of his religious belief or metaphysical philosophy, he lacks faith. For where faith is there is courage, there is fortitude, there is steadfastness and strength.

Light the Lamp of True Faith

The opinions of men are lightly to be considered, for they are changing with every new breeze of thought. They have very little part in the reality of things, being the bubbles of a surface effervescence. But behind all opinions there is the same human heart. The "godless" are they who are goodless, even though they may be members of churches and make a great profession of faith in God. The "godly" are they who are goodly even though they make no profession of religion. The complainers and bewailers are the faithless and unbelieving. Those who deny or belittle the power of good, and in their lives and actions affirm and magnify the power of evil, are the only real atheists.

Faith bestows that sublime courage that rises superior to the petty and selfish disappointments and troubles of life, that acknowledges no defeat except as a step to victory; that is strong to endure, patient to wait, and energetic to struggle. It perceives the benign law of Truth in all things, and is assured of the final triumph of the heart, and the kingly power of the mind.

Light up, then, the lamp of faith in your heart, and walk through the darkness guided by its illuminating rays. Its light is dim, and cannot be compared with the sunlight brilliance of knowledge, but it suffices to lead one safely through the mists of doubt and the black darkness of despair; along the narrow, thorny ways of sickness and sorrow, and over the treacherous planes of temptation and uncertainty. It enables man to ward off and outstrip the foul beasts that rage in the jungle of his heart, and to reach safely the open plains of a pure life and the mountain levels of conquest where the dim light of faith is no longer needed. For, leaving behind him all the darkness, all the doubt, error, and sorrow, he enters into a new consciousness and upon a higher round of life, works, and acts, and lives self-contained and peaceful, in the full and glorious light of knowledge.

Manliness, Womanliness and Sincerity

BEFORE A MAN CAN BE TRULY GODLY, he must be manly; before a woman can be truly godly, she must be womanly. There can be no true goodness apart from moral strength. Simpering, pretense, artificial behavior, flatteries, insincerities and smiling hypocrisies—let these things be forever destroyed and banished from our minds. Evil is inherently weak, ineffectual, and cowardly. Good is essentially strong, effective, and courageous.

In teaching men and women to be good, I teach them to be strong, free, self-reliant. They will greatly misunderstand me and the principles which I enunciate who imagine that because I teach gentleness, purity, and patience I teach the cultivation of an effeminate weakness. It is only the manly man and the womanly woman who can properly understand those divine qualities. No one is better equipped to achieve the Life Triumphant than they who, along with active moral qualities and a high sense of purity and honor, are also possessed of the strong animal nature of the normal man.

That animal force which, in various forms, surges within you, and which, in the hour of excitement, carries you blindly away, causing you to forget your higher nature and to forfeit your manly dignity and honor—that same force controlled, mastered, and rightly directed, will endow you with a divine strength by which you can achieve the highest, noblest, most blissful victories of true living.

The savage within you is to be scourged and disciplined into obedience. You are to be the master of your heart, your mind, yourself. Man is only weak and abject when he gives up the reins of government to the lower, instead of directing the lower by the higher. Your passions are to be your servants and slaves, not your masters. See that you keep them in their places, duly controlled and commanded, and they shall render you faithful, strong, and happy service.

You are not "vile." There is no part of your body or mind that is vile. Nature does not make mistakes.

The Universe is framed on Truth. All your functions, faculties, and powers are good, and to direct them rightly is wisdom, holiness, happiness; to direct them wrongly is folly, sin, and misery.

Be True to Yourself

Men waste themselves in excesses; in bad tempers, hatreds, gluttonies, and unworthy and unlawful pleasures, and then blame life. They should blame themselves.

A man should have more self-respect than to abuse his nature in any way. He should command himself always; should avoid excitement and hurry; should be too noble to give way to anger, to resent the actions and opinions of others, or fruitlessly to argue with an abusive and cantankerous assailant.

A quiet, unobtrusive, and unoffending dignity is the chief mark of a ripe and perfect manhood. Honor others and respect yourself. Choose your own path and walk it with a firm, unflinching step, but avoid a meddlesome interference with others. In the true man opposing qualities are blended and harmonized; a yielding kindness accompanies an unbending strength. He adapts himself gently and wisely to others without sacrificing the steadfast principles upon which his manhood is built. To have that iron strength that can go calmly to death rather than yield one jot of truth, along with that tender sympathy that can shield the weak and mistaken enemy, is to be manly with a divine manhood.

Be true to the dictates of your own conscience, and respect all who do the same, even though their conscience should lead them in a direction the reverse of your own. One of the most unmanly tendencies is to pity another because he chooses opinions or religion contrary to those of one's self. Why pity a man because he is an agnostic, or an atheist, or a Buddhist, or a Christian? Because he does not hold this opinion or that belief? Such pity should be rightly named contempt. It is the office of pity to feel for the weak, the afflicted, and the helpless.

Pity never says "I pity you"; it does kind deeds. It is superciliousness that professes pity for the strong, the self-reliant, for those who have the courage to mark out their own path and to walk it boldly. Why should he be forced to hold my opinion or yours? If what I say and do appeal to his reason and conscience as right, then he will be one with me and will work hand and hand with me. But if my work be not his work, he is nonetheless a man. He has his duty, though it not be my duty. When I meet one who is self-respecting, and who dares to think for himself, I will salute him as a man, and not harbor in my heart a contemptible pity for him, because, indeed, he rejects my conclusions.

If we are to be responsible, self-acting beings in a law-begotten universe, let us be masters of our own wills, and respect the free will of others. If we are to be strong and manly, let us be large-hearted and magnanimous. If we are to triumph over the miseries of life, let us rise superior to the pettiness of our nature.

Eliminate Weakness

Men weep in their weakness, and cry out in misery of heart and degradation of mind. How plain, then, is the way of emancipation; how sublime the task of triumph! Be master of yourself. Eliminate weakness. Exorcise the mocking fiend, selfishness, in whom is all weakness and wretchedness. Do not pander to unnatural cravings, to unlawful desires, or to morbid self-love and self-pity. Give them no quarter, but promptly stamp them out with disciplinary decision and strength.

A man should hold himself, as it were, in the hollow of his hand. He should be able to take up and to lay down. He should know how to use things, and not be used by them. He should neither be the helpless captive of luxury nor the whipped slave of want, but should be self-contained and self-sufficient, master of himself under all conditions. He must train and direct his will in the way of self-mastery which is the way of obedience—obedience to the law of his nature. Disobedience to law is the supreme evil in man, the source of all his sin and sorrow. In his ignorance he imagines he can triumph over law and subdue the wills of others. He thus destroys his power.

Man can triumph over his disobedience, over ignorance, sin, egotism, and lawlessness. He can conquer self; and herein lies his manly strength and divine power. He can comprehend the law of his being, and obey it as a child obeys the will of its father. He can sit the crowned king of all his functions and faculties, using them wisely in unselfish service, and not as instruments of selfishness and greed. There is no bad habit that he cannot uproot, no sin that he cannot subdue, no sorrow that he cannot comprehend and conquer. "Let a man then know his worth, and keep things under his feet. Let him not peep or steal, or skulk up and down with the air of a charity boy or an interloper, in the world which exists for him."

A manly self-reliance is not only compatible with, but is the accompaniment of, a divine humility. A man is only arrogant and egotistic when he usurps authority over others. He cannot claim nor exercise too great an authority over himself. Strong self-command, with gentle consideration for others, combine to make the truly manly man.

Conscious and Unconscious Hypocrisy

To begin with, a man must be honest, upright, sincere. Deceit is the blindest folly. Hypocrisy is the weakest thing on earth. In trying to deceive others, a man most of all deceives himself. A man should be so free from guile, meanness, and deceit as to be able to look everybody in the face with a clear, open, unflinching gaze, free from shame and confusion, and with no inward shrinking or misgivings. Without sincerity a man is but a hollow mask, and whatsoever work he attempts to do, it will be lifeless and ineffectual. Out of a hollow vessel nothing but the sound of hollowness can come; and from insincerity nothing but empty words can proceed.

Many are not consciously hypocrites, yet fall victims, thoughtlessly, to little insincerities which undermine happiness and destroy the moral fabric of their character. Some of these people go regularly to their place of worship. They pray daily, year after year, for a purer heart and life, yet come from their devotions to vilify an enemy, or, worse still, to ridicule or slander an absent friend for whom, when they meet him or her, they will have nothing but smiles and smooth words. The pitiful part of it is that they are totally unconscious of their insincerity, and when their friends desert them, they speak complainingly of the faithlessness and hollowness of the world, and of people generally, and tell you sadly that there are no true friends in this world.

Truly, for such there are no abiding friendships. For insincerity, even if not seen, is felt, and those who are incapable of bestowing trust and truth, cannot receive it. Be true to others, and others will be true to you. Think well of an enemy, and defend the absent friend. If you have lost faith in human nature, discover where you have gone wrong yourself.

The Words of Confucius

In the Confucian code of morals sincerity is one of the "Five Great Virtues," and Confucius thus speaks of it: "It is sincerity which places a crown upon your lives. Without it, our best actions would be valueless; the seemingly virtuous, mere hypocrites; and the shining light which dazzles us with its splendor, but a poor passing gleam ready to be extinguished by the slightest breath of passion....To be pure in mind, you must be free from self-deception—you must hate vice as you would a disagreeable odor, and love virtue as you would some beautiful object. There can be no self-respect without it, and this is why the superior man must be guarded in his hours of solitude.

"The worthless man secretly employs his idle moments in vicious acts, and there is no limit to his wickedness. In the presence of the pure he plays the hypocrite, and puts forward none but his good qualities. Yet how does this disguise hide him when his true character is revealed to the first scrutinizing glance?

"It has been said that there is a strict watch kept over that which is pointed at by many hands, and gazed at by many eyes. It is in solitude, then, that the upright man has the greatest reason to be guarded."

Sincerity Wins Hearts

Thus the sincere man does not do or say that which he would be ashamed of were it brought to light. His uprightness of spirit enables him to walk upright and confident among his fellow men. His presence is a strong protection, and his words are direct and powerful because they are true. Whatever may be his work, it prospers. Though he may not always please the ears of men, he wins their hearts; they rely on him, trust, and honor him.

Courage, self-reliance, sincerity, generosity and kindness—these are the virtues which constitute a robust manhood. Without them, a man is but clay in the hands of circumstances; a weak, wavering thing that cannot rise into the freedom and joy of a true life. Every young man should cultivate and foster these virtues, and as he succeeds in living them will he prepare to achieve the Life Triumphant.

I see coming upon the earth a new race of men and women—men who will be men indeed, strong, upright, noble; too wise to stoop to anger, uncleanness, strife, and hatred—women who would be women indeed, gentle, truthful, pure; too compassionate to stoop to gossip, slander, and deception. From their loins will proceed superior beings of the same noble type; and the dark fiends of error and evil will fall back at their approach. These noble men and women will regenerate the earth. They will dignify man, and vindicate nature, restoring humanity to love, happiness, and peace; and the life of victory over sin and sorrow will be established in the earth.

Energy and Power

HOW WONDERFUL is the universal energy! Never-tiring, inexhaustible, and apparently eternal in its operation, it moves in atom and in star, informing the fleeting shapes of time with its restless, glowing, pulsating power.

Man is a portion of this creative energy, and in him it manifests, through a combination of mental faculties, as affection, passion, intelligence, morality, reason, understanding, and wisdom. He is not merely a blind conductor of energy, but he consciously uses, controls, and directs it. Slowly, but with certainty, is he gaining control of the forces without, and is making them do obedient service. And just as surely will he gain control of the forces within—the subtle energies of thought—and direct them into channels of harmony and happiness.

Man's true place in the Cosmos is that of a king, not a slave, a commander under the law of Good and not a helpless tool in the reign of Evil. His own body and mind are the dual dominion over which he is to reign, a Lord of Truth, the master of himself, the wise user and controller of his store of pure, eternal, creative energy. Let him walk the earth unashamed, strong, valiant, tender, and kind; no longer prostrate in self-abasement, but walking erect in the dignity of perfect manhood; not groveling in selfishness and remorse, nor crying for pardon and mercy, but standing firm and free in the sublime majesty of a sinless life.

A New Era is Upon Us

Long has man regarded himself as vile, weak, and unworthy, and has been content to remain so. But in the new era which has just now burst upon the world, he is to make a glorious discovery that he is pure, powerful, and noble when he rises up and wills. The rising up is not against any outward enemy; not against neighbor, nor governments, nor laws, nor spirits, nor principalities, but against the ignorance, folly, and misery which beset him in the dominion of his own mind. For it is only by ignorance and folly that man is slavish; by knowledge and wisdom his kingdom is restored.

Let them who will, preach man's weakness and

helplessness, but I will teach his strength and power. I write for men, not for babes; for those who are eager to learn, and earnest to achieve; for those who will put away (for the world's good) a petty personal indulgence, a selfish desire, a mean thought, and live on as though it were not, without craving and regret. The Truth is not for the frivolous and the thoughtless. The Life Triumphant is not for triflers and loiterers.

Your Weakness is Misdirected Strength

Man is a master. If he were not, he could not act contrary to law. Thus his so-called weakness is an indication of strength; his sin is the inversion of his capacity for holiness. For what is his weakness and sin but misdirected energy, misapplied power? In this sense, the wrongdoer is strong, not weak; but he is ignorant, and exerts his strength in wrong directions instead of right, against the law of things instead of with it.

Suffering is the recoil of misdirected strength. The bad man becomes good by reversing his conduct. If you are weeping over your sins, cease to commit those sins and establish yourself in their opposing virtues. It is thus that weakness is converted into strength, helplessness into power, and suffering into bliss. By turning his energies from the old channels of vice, and directing them into the new channels of virtue, the sinner becomes a saint.

Energy—The Law of Compensation

While the universal energy may be unlimited, in particular forms its sum is strictly limited. A man is possessed of a given amount of energy, and he can use it or misuse it, can conserve and concentrate it, or dissipate and disperse it. Power is concentrated energy; wisdom is that energy adapted to beneficent ends. He is the man of influence and power who directs all his energies towards one great purpose, and patiently works and waits for its fulfillment, sacrificing his desires in other and more pleasant directions. He is the man of folly and weakness who, thinking chiefly of pleasure, gratifies the desire of the hour, or follows the whim and impulse of the moment, and so drifts thoughtlessly into peevishness and poverty of mind.

The energy used in one direction is not available for use in other directions; this is a universal law both in mind and matter. Emerson calls it "the law of compensation." Gain in a given direction necessitates loss in its opposite direction. The force placed in one scale is deducted from the other scale. Nature is always endeavoring to strike a balance. The energy which is dissipated in idleness is not given to work. The pleasure-seeker cannot also be a Truth-seeker.

The force wasted in a fit of bad temper is drawn from the man's store of virtue, particularly the virtue of patience. Spiritually, this law of compensation is the law of sacrifice. Selfish pleasure must be sacrificed if purity is to be gained; hatred must be yielded up if love is to be acquired; vice must be renounced if virtue is to be embraced.

Comparing the Foolish and Earnest

Earnest men soon discover that if they are to accomplish anything that is successful, strong, and enduring, in worldly, intellectual, or spiritual channels, they must curb their desires, and sacrifice much that seems sweet; yea, even much that seems important.

Hobbies, bodily and mental indulgences, enticing companionships, alluring pleasures, and all work that does not tend to some central purpose in his life must be sacrificed by the man of strong resolve. He opens his eyes to the fact that time and energy are strictly limited, and so he economizes the one and concentrates the other.

Foolish men waste their energies in swinish ease

and gluttonous indulgence, in frivolous pleasures and empty talk, in hateful thoughts and irritable outbursts of passion, in vain controversy and meddlesome interference. They then complain that many are more "fortunately" equipped than they are for a useful, successful, or great life, and they envy their honored neighbor who has sacrificed self to duty, and has devoted all his energies to the faithful performance of the business of his life.

"He who is just, speaks the truth, and does what is his own business, him the world will hold dear." Let a man attend to his own business, concentrating all his energies upon the perfect accomplishment of the task of his life, not stepping aside to condemn or interfere with the duties of others, and he will find life simple, strong, and happy.

The Lower Must Be Sacrificed

The universe is girt with goodness and strength, and it protects the strong and the good. Evil and weakness are self-destructive. Dissipation is annihilation. All nature loves strength. I see no inherent cruelty in "the survival of the fittest." It is a spiritual as well as a natural law. The stronger qualities of the beast are the fittest to evolve a higher type. The nobler moral qualities in man are his emancipators, and it is well that they should dominate and ultimately crush out the ignoble tendencies.

Most certain it is that he who gives dominion to the lower, courts destruction, and does not survive, either in the struggle of life without or the battle of Truth within. The life given to the lower is lost to the higher; yea, it is finally lost also to the lower, and so all is lost, for evil is ultimately nothingness. But the life given to the higher is preserved, and is not lost to anything, for, while it sacrifices much that the world holds precious, it does not sacrifice anything that is precious in reality.

The untrue and worthless must perish, and he who consecrates himself to the good and the true is content that they should perish, and so at last he stands where sacrifice ends, and all is gain—such a one survives in the struggle of life without, and he conquers in the battle of Truth within.

Your Strength is Within You

First, then, be strong. Strength is the firm basis on which is built the temple of the Triumphant Life. Without a central motive and fixed resolve, your life will be a poor, weak, drifting, unstable thing. Let the act of the moment be governed by the deep abiding purpose of the heart. You will act differently at different times, but the act will not be wrong if the heart is right. You may fall and go astray at times, especially under great stress, but you will quickly regain yourself, and you will grow wiser and stronger, thereby, so long as you guide yourself by the moral compass within, and do not throw it away to gratify indulgence and give yourself up to uncertain drifting.

Follow your conscience. Be true to your convictions. Do at the moment what you regard as right, and put away all procrastination, vacillation, and fear. If you are convinced that in the performance of your duty under certain circumstances the severest measures are necessary, carry out those measures, and let there be no uncertainty about it. Err on the side of strength rather than weakness. The measures you adopt may not be the best, but if they are the best you know, then your plain duty is to carry them out. By so doing you will discover the better way, if you are anxious for progress, and are willing to learn. Deliberate beforehand, but in the time of action do not hesitate.

Lift Your Thoughts Upward

Avoid anger and stubbornness, lust and greed.

The angry man is the weak man. The stubborn man, who refuses to learn or mend his ways, is the foolish man. He grows old in folly, and grey hairs do not bring him reverence or honor. The sensualist has energy for pleasure only, and reserves none for manliness and self-respect. The greedy man is blind to the nobility of human nature and the glory of a true life; he spends his energies in perpetuating the miseries of hell, instead of enjoying the happiness of heaven.

Your strength is with you, and you can spend it in burrowing downward or in climbing upward. You can dissipate it in selfishness or conserve it in goodness. The same energy will enable you to become a beast or a god. The course along which you direct it will determine its effect. Do not think the thought, "My mind is weak," but convert weakness into strength, and energy into power by redirecting your mental forces. Turn your thoughts into noble channels. Put away vain longings and foolish regrets; abolish complaint and self-condolence, and have no dalliance with evil. Lift your face upward. Rise up in your divine strength, and spurn from your mind and life all meanness and weakness. Do not live the false life of a whining slave, but live the true life of a conquering master.

Self-Control and Happiness

When mental energy is allowed to follow the line of least resistance, and to fall into easy channels, it is called weakness. When it is gathered, focused, and forced into upward and different directions, it becomes power; and this concentration of energy and acquisition of power is brought about by means of self-control.

In speaking of self-control, one is easily misunderstood. It should not be associated with a destructive repression, but with a constructive expression. The process is not one of death, but of life. It is a divine and masterly transmutation in which the weak is converted into the strong, the coarse into the fine, and the base into the noble; in which virtue takes the place of vice, and dark passion is lost in bright intellectuality.

The man who merely smothers up and hides away

his real nature, without any higher object in view than to create a good impression upon others concerning his character, is practicing hypocrisy and not self-control. As the mechanic transmutes coal into gas, and water into steam, and then concentrates and utilizes the finer forces for the comfort and convenience of others, so the man who intellectually practices self-control transmutes his lower inclinations into the finer qualities of intelligence and mortality to the increase of his own and the world's happiness.

A man is happy, wise, and great in the measure that he controls himself; he is wretched, foolish, and mean in the measure that he allows his animal nature to dominate his thoughts and actions.

He who controls himself controls his life, his circumstances, his destiny, and wherever he goes he carries his happiness with him as an abiding possession. He who does not control himself, is controlled by passions, by his circumstances, and his fate; and if he cannot gratify the desire of the moment, he is disappointed and miserable. He depends for his fitful happiness on external things.

Transmutation Demands Effort and Patience

There is no force in the universe which can be

annihilated or lost. Energy is transformed, but not destroyed. To shut the door on old and bad habits is to open it to new and better ones. Renunciation precedes regeneration. Every self-indulgence, every forbidden pleasure, every hateful thought renounced is transformed into something more purely and permanently beautiful. Where debilitating excitements are cut off, there spring up rejuvenating joys. The seed dies that the flower may appear; the grub perishes, but the dragonfly comes forth.

Truly, the transformation is not instantaneous; nor is the transition a pleasant and painless process. Nature demands effort and patience as the price of growth. In the march of progress, every victory is contested with struggle and pain; but the victory is achieved, and it abides. The struggle passes; the pain is temporary only. To demolish a firmly fixed habit, to break up a mental tendency that has become automatic with long use, and to force into birth and growth a fine characteristic or lofty virtue—to accomplish this necessitates a painful metamorphosis, a transitional period of darkness, to pass through which patience and endurance are required.

This is where men fail. This is where they slip back into their old, easy, animal ruts, and abandon self-control as too strenuous and severe. Thus they fall short of permanent happiness, and the life of triumph over evil is hidden from their eyes.

Self-Control Brings Happiness

The permanent happiness which men seek in dissipation, excitement, and abandonment to unworthy pleasure is found only in the life which reverses all this—the life of self-control. So far as a man deviates from perfect self-command, just so far does he fall short of perfect happiness. He sinks into misery and weakness, the lowest limit of which is madness, entire lack of mental control, the condition of irresponsibility. In so far as a man approximates to perfect self-command, just so near does he approach to perfect happiness, and rise into joy and strength. So glorious are the possiblities of such divine manhood, that no limit can be set to its grandeur and bliss.

If a man will understand how intimately, yea, how inseparably, self-control and happiness are associated, he has but to look into his own heart, and upon the world around, to find there the joy destroying effects of uncontrolled tendencies. Looking upon the lives of men and women, he will perceive how the hasty word, the bitter retort, the act of deception, the blind prejudice and foolish resentment bring wretchedness and even ruin in their train. Looking into his own life, what days of consuming remorse, of restless anxiety, and of crushing sorrow rise up before his mind—periods of intense suffering through which he has passed through lack of self-control.

But in the right life, the well-governed life, the victorious life, all these things pass away. New conditions obtain, and purer, more espiritual instruments are employed for the achievements of happy ends. There is no more remorse, because there is no more wrong-doing. There is no more anxiety, because there is no more selfishness. There is no more sorrow, because Truth is the source of action.

The Lack of Self-Control Brings Remorse

The much desired thing which self pursues with breathless and uncontrolled eagerness, yet fails to overtake, comes unbidden, and begs to be admitted, to him who works and waits in perfect self-command. Hatred, impatience, greed, self-indulgence, vain ambitions, and blind desires—the instruments by which self shapes its ill-finished existence, what clumsy tools they are, and how ignorant and unskillful are they who employ them! Love, patience, kindness, self-discipline, transmuted ambitions, and chastened desires—instruments of Truth, by which is shaped a well-finished existence, what perfect tools they are, and how wise and skillful are they who use them!

Whatsoever is gained by feverish haste and selfish desire is attained in fuller measure by quietness and renunciation. Nature will not be hastened. She brings all perfection in due season. Truth will not be commanded. He has his conditions and must be obeyed. Nothing is more superfluous than haste and anger.

A man has to learn he cannot command things, but that he can command himself; that he cannot coerce the wills of others, but that he can mold and master his own will: and things serve him who serve Truth. People seek guidance of him who is master of himself.

Wisdom Found in Self-Control

It is a little understood, yet simple and profound truth, that the man who cannot command himself under the severest external stress is unfit to guide others or to control affairs. It is the fundamental principle in the moral and political teachings of Confucius that, before attempting to govern affairs, a man should learn to govern himself. Men who habitually give way, under pressure, to hysterical suspicions, outbursts of resentment, and explosions of anger, are unfit for weighty responsibilities and lofty duties, and usually fail, sooner or later, even in the ordinary duties of life, such as the management of their own family or business. Lack of self-control is foolishness, and folly cannot take precedence over wisdom.

He who is learning how to subdue and control his turbulent, wandering thoughts is becoming wiser every day. Though for a time the Temple of Joy will not be completed, he will gather strength in laying its foundations and building its walls; and the day will come when, like a wise master-builder, he will rest at peace in the beautiful habitation which he has built. Wisdom inheres in self-control and in wisdom is "pleasantness and peace."

Self-Control Intensifies Enjoyment

The life of self-control is no barren deprivation, no wilderness of monotony. Renunciation there is, but it is a renunciation of the ephemeral and false in order that the abiding and true may be realized. Enjoyment is not cut off; it is intensified. Enjoyment is life; it is the slavish desire for it that kills. Is there anywhere a more miserable man than he who is always longing for some new sensation? Is there anywhere a more blessed being than he who, by self-control, is satisfied, calm, and enlightened? Who has most of physical life and joy—the glutton, the drunkard, and the sensualist who lives for pleasure only, or the temperate man who holds his body in subjection, considering its needs and obeying its uses?

I was once eating a ripe, juicy apple as it came from the tree, and a man near me said, "I would give anything if I could enjoy an apple like that." I asked, "Why can't you?" His answer was, "I have drunk whiskey and smoked tobacco until I have lost all enjoyment in such things." In pursuit of elusive enjoyments, men lose the abiding joys of life.

And as he who controls his senses has most of physical life, joy, and strength, so he who controls his thoughts has most of spiritual life, bliss, and power. For not only happiness, but knowledge and wisdom also are revealed by self-control. As the avenues of ignorance and selfishness are closed, the open gates of knowledge and enlightenment appear. Virtue attained is knowledge gained. The pure mind is an enlightened mind. He has well-being who controls himself well.

There is No Dullness in Self-Control

I hear men speak of the "monotony of goodness." If looking for things in the spirit which one has given up in the letter were "goodness," then indeed would it be monotonous. The man of self-control does not merely give up his base pleasures, he abandons all longing for them. He presses forward, and does not look back; and fresh beauties, new glories, sublimer vistas await him at every step.

I am astonished at the revelations which lie hidden in self-control; I am captivated by the infinite variety of Truth. I am filled with joy at the grandeur of the prospect; I am gladdened by its splendor and its peace.

Along the way of self-control there is the joy of victory; the consciousness of expanding and increasing power; the acquisition of the imperishable riches of divine knowledge; and the abiding bliss of service to humankind. Even he who travels only a portion of the way will develop a strength, achieve a success, and experience a joy which the idle and the thoughtless cannot know. And he who goes all the way will become a spiritual conqueror; he will triumph over all evil, and will blot it out. He will gaze with enrapt vision upon the majesty of the Cosmic Order, and will enjoy the immortality of Truth.

Simplicity and Freedom

YOU HAVE KNOWN what it is to be physically encumbered by some superfluous load. You have experienced the happy relief of dispensing with such a load. Your experience illustrates the difference between a life burdened with a complexity of desires, beliefs, and speculations, and one rendered simple and free by the satisfaction of its natural needs, and a calm contemplation of the facts of existence, eliminating all argument and speculation.

There are those who cumber their drawers, cupboards, and rooms with rubbish and clutter. To such an extent is this carried sometimes, that the house cannot be properly cleaned, and vermin swarms. There is no use for the rubbish, but they will not part with it, even though by so doing, they would also get rid of the vermin. But they like to think that it is there; like to feel that they have got it, especially if they are convinced that nobody else has its like. They reason that it may be of some use someday; or it may become valuable; or it brings up old associations which they occasionally resuscitate and take a paradoxical pleasure in sorrowing over.

In a sweet, methodical, well-managed house, such superfluities, bringing with them dirt, discomfort, and care, are not allowed to accumulate. Or should they have accumulated, they are gathered up and consigned to the fire and the trash bin, when it is decided to cleanse and restore the house, and give it light, comfort, and freedom.

In a like manner men hoard up in their minds mental rubbish and clutter, cling tenaciously to it, and fear its loss. Insatiate desires; thirsty cravings for unlawful and unnatural pleasures; conflicting beliefs about miracles, gods, angels, demons, and interminable theological complexities, hypothesis is piled upon hypothesis, speculation is added to speculation, until the simple, beautiful, all-sufficient facts of life are lost to sight and knowledge beneath the metaphysical pile.

The Simplified Life of Love

Simplicity consists in being rid of this painful

confusion of desires and superfluity of opinions, and adhering only to that which is permanent and essential.

And what is permanent in life? What is essential? Virtue alone is permanent; character is essential. So simple is life when it is freed from all superfluities and rightly understood and lived that it can be reduced to a few unmistakable, easy-to-understand, though hard-to-practice principles. And all great minds have so simplified life.

Buddha reduced it to eight virtues, in the practice of which he declared that men would acquire perfect enlightenment. And these eight virtues he reduced to one, which he called *compassion*.

Confucius taught that the perfection of knowledge was contained in five virtues, and these he expressed in one which he called *Reciprocity*, or *Sympathy*.

Jesus reduced the whole of life to the principle of *Love*. Compassion, Sympathy, Love, these three are identical. How simple they are, too! Yet I cannot find a man who fully understands the depths and heights of these virtues, for who so fully understood them would embody them in practice. He would be complete, perfect, divine. There would be nothing lacking in him of knowledge, virtue, and wisdom.

It is only when a man sets earnestly to work to

order his life in accordance with the simple precepts of virtue, that he discovers what piles of mental rubbish he has hoarded up, and which he is now compelled to throw away. The exactions, too, which such a course of conduct make upon his faith, endurance, patience, kindness, humility, reason, and strength of will, are, until the mind approaches the necessary condition of purity and simplicity, painful in their severity. The clearing-out process, whether of one's mind, home, or place of business, is not a light and easy one, but it ends in comfort and repose.

The Wise Have a Few Simple Rules

All complexities of detail, whether in things material or mental, are reducible to a few fundamental laws or principles by virtue of which they exist and are regulated. Wise men govern their lives by a few simple rules. A life governed by the central principle of love will be found to be divinely consistent in all its details. Every thought, word, act, will fall into proper place, and there will be no conflict and confusion.

"What," asked the learned man of the Buddhist saint who had acquired a wide reputation for sanctity and wisdom—"what is the most fundamental thing in Buddhism?" The saint replied, "The most fundamental thing in Buddhism is to cease from evil and to learn to do good." "I did not ask you," said the learned man, "to tell me what every child of three knows. I want you to tell me what is the most profound, the most subtle, and the most important thing in Buddhism." "The most profound, the most subtle, the most important thing in Buddhism," said the saint, "is to cease from evil and to learn to do well. It is true that a child of three may know it, but grey-haired old men fail to put it into practice."

The commentator then goes on to say that the learned man did not want facts; he did not want Truth. He wanted to be given some subtle metaphysical speculation which would give rise to another speculation, and then to another and another, and so afford him an opportunity of bringing into play the wonderful intellect of which he was so proud.

The Wise Fall Back on Simple Virtues

A member of a philosophical school once proudly said to me, "Our system of metaphysics is the most perfect and the most complicated in the world." I discovered how complicated it was by becoming involved in it and then pursuing the process of disentanglement back to the facts of life, simplicity, and freedom.

I have since learned how better to utilize my energy and occupy my time in the pursuit and practice of those virtues that are firm and sure, rather than to waste it in the spinning of the pretty but unsubstantial threads of metaphysical cobwebs.

But while regarding with disfavor assumption and pride, and that vanity which mistakes its own hypothesis for reality, I set no premium on ignorance and stupidity. Learning is a good thing. As an end in itself, as a possession to be proud of, it is a dead thing; but as a means to the high ends of human progress and human good it becomes a living power. Accompanied with a lowly mind, it is a powerful instrument for good.

The Buddhist saint was no less learned than his proud questioner, but he was more simple and wise. Even hypotheses will not lead us astray if they are perceived as mere hypotheses and are not confounded with facts. Yet the wisest men dispense with all hypotheses, and fall back on the simple practice of virtue. They thus become divine, and arrive at the acme of simplicity, enlightenment, and emancipation.

To arrive at the freedom and joy of simplicity, one must not think less, he must think more; only the thinking must be set to a high and useful purpose, and must be concentrated upon the facts and duties of life, instead of dissipated in unprofitable theorizing.

Simplicity Becomes Greatness

A life of simplicity is simple in all its parts because the heart which governs it has become pure and strong; because it is centered and rested in Truth. Harmful luxuries in food and vain superfluities in dress; exaggerations of speech and insincerities of action; thoughts that tend to intellectual display and empty speculation—all these are set aside in order that virtue may be better understood and more earnestly embraced. The duties of life are undertaken in a spirit from which self is eliminated, and they become transfigured with a new and glorious light, even the light of Truth. The great fundamental facts of life, heretofore hidden from knowledge, are plainly revealed, and the Eternal Verities, about which the wordy theorizers can only guess and argue, become substantial possessions.

The simple-hearted, the true-hearted, the virtuous and wise, are no longer troubled with doubts and fears about the future and the unknown and unknowable. They take their stand upon the duty of the hour, and on the known and the knowable. They do not barter away the actual for the hypothetical. They find in virtue an abiding security. They find in Truth an illuminating light which, while it reveals to them the true order of the facts of life, throws a halo of divine promise about the abyss of the unknown; and so they are at rest.

Simplicity works untrammelled, and becomes greatness and power. Suspicions, deceptions, impurities, despondencies, bewailings, doubts, and fears—all these are cast away, left behind and ignored, and the freed man, strong, self-possessed, calm, and pure, works in unclouded assurance, and inhabits heavenly planes.

Right Thinking and Repose

LIFE IS A COMBINATION OF HABITS, some baneful, some beneficent, all of which take their rise in the one habit of thinking. The thought makes the man; therefore right-thinking is the most important thing in life. The essential difference between a wise man and a fool is that the wise man controls his thinking, the fool is controlled by it. A wise man determines how and what he shall think, and does not allow external things to divert his thought from the main purpose. But a fool is carried captive by every tyrant thought as it is aroused within him by external things, and he goes through life the helpless tool of impulse, whim, and passion.

Careless, slovenly thinking, commonly called thoughtlessness, is the companion of failure, wrongdoing, and wretchedness. Nothing, no prayers, no religious ceremonies, not even acts of charity, can make up for wrong-thinking. Only right-thinking can rectify a wrong life. Only the right attitude of mind towards men and things can bring repose and peace.

The Triumphant Life is only for him whose heart and intellect are attuned to lofty virtue. He must make his thought logical, sequential, harmonious, symmetrical. He must mold and shape his thinking to fixed principles, and thereby establish his life on the sure foundation of knowledge. He must not merely be kind, he must be intelligently kind; must know why he is kind. His kindness must be an invariable quality, and not an intermittent impulse interspersed with fits of resentment and acts of harshness. He must not merely be virtuous under virtuous circumstances; his virtue must be of a kind that shall continue to shine with unabated light when he is assailed with vicious circumstances. He must not allow himself to be hurled from the throne of divine manhood by the shocks of fate or the praise and blame of those around him. Virtue must be his abiding habitation; his refuge from the whirlwind and the storm.

And virtue is not only of the heart; it is of the intellect also; and without this virtue of the intellect, the virtue of the heart is imperiled. Reason, like passion, has its vices. Metaphysical speculations are the riot of the intellect, as sensuality is the riot of the affections. The highest flights of speculation—pleasing as they are—reveal no place of rest, and the strained mind must return to facts and moral principles to find that truth which it seeks. As the soaring bird returns for refuge and rest to its nest in the rock, so must the speculative thinker return to the rock of virtue for surety and peace.

The Extent of Knowledge is Small

The intellect must be trained to comprehend the principles of virtue, and to understand all that is involved in their practice. Its energies must be restrained from wasteful indulgence in vain subtleties, and be directed in the path of righteousness and the way of wisdom. The thinker must distinguish, in his own mind, between reality and assumption. He must discover the extent of his actual knowledge. He must know what he knows. He must also know what he does not know. He must learn to discriminate between belief and knowledge, error and Truth.

In his search for the right attitude of mind which perceives truth, and works out a wise and radiant life, he must be more logical than logic, more merciless in exposing the errors of his own mind than the most sarcastic logician is in exposing the errors of the minds of others. After pursuing this course of discrimination for a short time, he will be astonished to find how small is the extent of his actual knowledge; yet he will be gladdened by its possession, for small as it is, it is the pure gold of knowledge. And what is better, to have a few grains of gold hidden away in tons of ore, where it is useless, or to extract the gold and throw away the ore?

As the miner sifts away bushels of dull earth to find the sparkling diamond, so the spiritual miner, the true thinker, sifts away from his mind the accumulation of opinions, beliefs, speculations, and assumptions to find the bright jewel of Truth which bestows upon its possessor wisdom and enlightenment.

And the concentrated knowledge which is ultimately brought to light by this sifting process is found to be so closely akin to virtue that it cannot be divided from it, cannot be set apart as something different.

Knowledge Leads to Virtue

In his search for knowledge Socrates discovered virtue. The divine maxims of the Great Teachers are maxims of virtue. When knowledge is separated from virtue, wisdom is lost. What a man practices, that he knows. What he does not practice, that he does not know. A man may write treatises or preach sermons on Love, but if he treats his family harshly, or thinks spitefully of his enemy, what knowledge has he concerning Love?

In the heart of the man of knowledge there dwells a silent and abiding compassion that shames the fine words of the noisy theorist. He only knows what peace is whose heart is free from hatred, who lives in peace with all. Cunning definitions of virtue only serve to deepen ignorance when they proceed from vice-stained lips. Knowledge has a deeper source than the mere memorizing of information. That knowledge is divine which proceeds from acquaintance with virtue. The humility which purges the intellect of its empty opinions and vain assumptions also fortifies it with a searching insight and invincible power. There is a divine logic which is indistinguished from love. The reply, "He that is without sin among you, let him cast the first stone," is unanswerable logic. It is also perfect love.

The Right and Wrong Thinker

The wrong thinker is known by his vices; the right thinker is know by his virtues. Troubles and unrest assail the mind of the wrong thinker, and he experiences no abiding repose. He imagines that others can injure, snub, cheat, degrade and ruin him. Knowing nothing of the protection of virtue, he seeks the protection of self, and takes refuge in suspicion, spite, resentment, and retaliation, and is burnt in the fire of his own vices.

When slandered, he slanders in return; when accused, he recriminates; when assailed, he turns upon his adversary with double fierceness. "I have been treated unjustly!" exclaims the wrong thinker, and then abandons himself to resentment and misery. Having no insight and unable to distinguish evil from good, he cannot see that his own evil, and not his neighbor's, is the cause of all his trouble.

The right thinker is not concerned with thoughts about self and self-protection, and the wrong actions of others towards him cannot cause him trouble or unrest. He cannot think—"This man has wronged me." He perceives that no wrong can reach him but by his own evil deeds. He understands that his welfare is at his own hands, and thus none but himself can rob him of repose. Virtue is his protection, and retaliation is foreign to him. He holds himself steadfastly in peace, and resentment cannot enter his heart. Temptation does not find him unprepared, and it assails in vain the strong citadel of his mind. Abiding in virtue, he abides in strength and peace.

The right-thinker has discovered and acquired the right attitude of mind toward men and things—the attitude of a profound and loving repose. And this is not resignation, it is wisdom. It is not indifference, but watchful and penetrating insight. He has comprehended the facts of life; he sees things as they are. He does not overlook the particulars of life, but reads them in the light of cosmic law; sees them in their right relations as portions of the universal scheme. He sees the universe is upheld by justice. He watches, but does not engage in, the petty quarrels and fleeting strifes of men. He cannot be partisan. His sympathy is with all. He cannot favor one portion more than another. He knows that good will ultimately conquer in the world, as it has conquered in individuals; that there is a sense in which good already conquers, for evil defeats itself.

Good is not defeated; justice is not set aside. Whatever man may do, justice reigns, and its eternal throne cannot be assailed and threatened, much less conquered and overthrown. This is the source of the true thinker's abiding repose. Having become righteous, he perceives the righteous law. Having acquired

Love, he understands the Eternal Love. Having conquered evil, he knows that good is supreme.

The Life Triumphant is for the Pure

He is only the true thinker whose heart is free from hatred, lust, and pride; who looks out upon the world through eyes washed free from evil; whose bitterest enemy arouses no enmity, but only tender pity in his heart; who does not talk vainly about things of which he has no knowledge, and whose heart is always at peace.

And by this a man may know that his thoughts are in accordance with the Truth—that there is no more bitterness in his heart, that malice has departed from him; that he loves where he formerly condemned.

A man may be learned, but if he is not wise he will not be a true thinker. Not by learning will a man triumph over evil; not by much study will he overcome sin and sorrow. Only by conquering himself will he conquer evil; only by practicing righteousness will he put an end to sorrow.

Not for the clever, nor the learned, nor the self-confident is the Life Triumphant, but for the pure, the virtuous, the wise. The former achieve their particular success in life, but the latter alone achieve the Great

Success, a success so invincible and complete that even an apparent defeat shines with added victory.

Virtue cannot be shaken; virtue cannot be confounded; virtue cannot be overthrown. He who thinks in accordance with virtue, who acts righteously, whose mind is the servant of truth, he it is who conquers in life and in death. For virtue must triumph, and Righteousness and Truth are the pillars of the universe.

Calmness and Resource

HE WHO HAS TRUTH is always self-possessed. Hurry and excitement, anxiety and fear have no place in the purified mind and the true life. Self-conquest results in perpetual calm. Calmness is the radiant light which adds a luster to all the virtues. Like the nimbus round the head of the saint, it surrounds virtue with its shining halo. Without calmness a man's greatest strength is but a kind of exaggerated weakness. Where is a man's spiritual strength—where indeed, is his ordinary manly strength—who loses his balance with almost every petty disturbance from without? And what enduring influence can a man have who forgets himself in sinful abandonment or unseemly rage in the hour of temptation and crisis?

The virtuous put a check upon themselves, and

set a watch upon their passions and emotions. In this way they gain possession of the mind, and gradually acquire calmness. And as they acquire calmness, they acquire influence, power, greatness, abiding joy, and fullness and completeness of life.

Those who do not put a check upon themselves, whose emotions and passions are their masters, who crave excitement and race after unholy pleasures—these are not yet fit for a life of joyful victory, and can neither appreciate nor receive the beautiful jewel of calmness. Such may pray for peace with their lips, but they do not desire it in their hearts; or the word "peace" may only mean to them another kind of periodic pleasure which they desire to enjoy.

In the life of calm there are no fitful periods of sinful excitement followed by reactionary hours of sorrow and remorse. There are no foolish elations followed by equally foolish depressions; no degrading actions followed by misery and loss of self-respect. All these things are put away, and what remains is Truth, and Truth is forever encircled with peace. The calm life is new unbroken bliss. Duties which are irksome to the ungoverned are things of joy to the calm man. Indeed, in the calm life, the word "duty" receives a new meaning. It is no longer opposed to happiness, but it is one with happiness. The calm man, the right-seeing man, cannot separate joy from duty. Such separation belongs to the mind and life of the pleasure-hunter and lover of excitement.

Peace Is Gained by Conquering Self

Calmness is difficult to attain because men cling blindly to the lower disturbances of the mind for the passing pleasure which these disturbances afford. Even sorrow is sometimes selfishly gloated over as a kind of occasional luxury. But though difficult to attain, the way which leads to its attainment is simple. It consists of abandoning all those excitements and disturbances which are opposed to it, and fortifying one's self in these steadfast virtues, which do not change with changing events and circumstances, which have no violent reactions, and which therefore bestow perpetual satisfaction and abiding peace.

He only finds peace who conquers himself, who strives, day by day, after self-possession, greater self-control, greater calmness of mind. One can only be a joy to himself and a blessing to others in the measure that he has command of himself; and such self-command is gained only by persistent practice. A man must conquer his weaknesses by daily effort. He must understand them and study how to eliminate them from his character. If he continues to strive, not giving way, he will gradually become victorious. Each little victory gained (though there is a sense in which no victory can be called little) will be so much more calmness acquired and added to his character as an eternal possession.

He will thus make himself strong, capable, and blessed, fit to perform his duties faultlessly, and to meet all events with an untroubled spirit. But even if he does not, in this life, reach that supreme calm which no shock can disturb, he will become sufficiently self-possessed and pure to enable him to fight the battle of life fearlessly, and to leave the world a little richer for having known the goodness of his presence.

By constantly overcoming self, a man gains a knowledge of the subtle intricacies of his mind; and it is this divine knowledge which enables him to become established in calmness. Without self-knowledge there can be no abiding peace of mind, and those who are carried away by tempestuous passions cannot approach the holy place where calmness reigns. The weak man is like one who, having mounted a fiery steed, allows it to run away with him, and carry him withersoever it wills. The strong man is like one who, having mounted the steed, governs it with a masterly hand, and makes it go in whatever direction, and at whatever speed he commands.

Calmness is the Result of Self-Control

Calmness is the crowning beauty of a character that has become, or is becoming, divine, and is restful and peace-giving to all who come in contact with it. Those who are still in their weakness and doubt, find the presence of the calm mind restful to their troubled minds, inspiring to their faltering feet, and rich with healing and comfort in the hour of sorrow. For he who is strong to overcome self is strong to help others. He who has conquered soul-weariness is strong to help the weary on the way.

That calmness of mind, which is not disturbed or overthrown by trials and emergencies, or by the accusations, slanders, and misrepresentations of others, is born of great spiritual strength. It is the true indication of an enlightened and wise understanding. The calm mind is the exalted mind. Divinely gentle and externally strong is that man who does not lose his serenity, nor forget his peace when falsehoods and indignities are heaped upon him. Such calmness is the perfect flower of self-control. It has been slowly and laboriously gained, by patiently passing through the fires of suffering, by subjecting the mind to a long process of purification.

Calmness is Power

The calm man has discovered the spring of both happiness and knowledge within himself, and it is a spring than can never run dry. His powers are at his full command, and there is no limit to his resources. In whatever direction he employs his energies, he will manifest originality and power. And this is so because he deals with things as they are, and not with mere opinions about things. If he has any opinions left, he is no longer enamored of them, but sees them as they are—mere opinions, and therefore of no intrinsic value. He has abolished egotism, and, by obedience to law, has become one with the power in nature and the universe. His resources are untrammeled by selfishness; his energies unhindered by pride.

There is a sense in which he has ceased to regard anything as his own. Even his virtues belong to Truth, and not exclusively to his person. He has become a conscious principle of Cosmic Power, and is no longer a mean, dwarfed thing, seeking petty personal ends. And having put away self, he has put away the greed, the misery, the troubles and fears which belong to self. He acts calmly, and accepts all consequences with equal calmness. He is efficient and accurate, and perceives all that is involved in any undertaking. He does not work blindly; he knows that there is no chance of favor.

Calmness is Cosmic Perfection

The mind of the calm man is like the surface of a still lake; it reflects life and the things of life truly. Whereas, the troubled mind, like the troubled surface of the lake, gives back a distorted image of all things which fall upon it. Gazing into the serene depths within him, the self-conquered man sees a just reflection of the universe. He sees the Cosmic Perfection; sees the equity in his own lot. Even those things which are regarded by the world as unjust and grievous (and which formerly appeared so to him) are now known to be the effects of his own past deeds, and are therefore joyfully accepted as portions of the perfect whole. Thus his calmness remains with him with its illimitable fund of resource in joy and enlightenment.

The calm man succeeds where the disturbed man fails. He is fit to deal with any external difficulty, who has successfully grappled with the most intricate difficulties and problems within his own heart. He who has succeeded in governing the within is best equipped to govern the without. The calm mind perceives a difficulty in all its bearings and understands best how to meet it. The disturbed mind is the lost mind. It has become blind, seeing not whither to go, but only feeling its own unhappiness and fear.

The resources of the calm man are superior to all incidents which may befall him. Nothing can alarm him, nothing can find him unprepared, nothing can shake his strong and steadfast mind. Wheresoever duty may call him, there will his strength manifest itself; there will his mind, free from the frictions of self, exhibit its silent and patient power. Whether he be engaged in things worldly or things spiritual, he will do his work with concentrated vigor and penetrating insight.

Merging into the Cosmic Will

Calmness means that the mind is harmoniously adjusted, perfectly poised. All its extremes once so antagonistic and painful are reconciled, merged into one grand central principle with which the mind has identified itself. It means that the runaway passions are tamed and subjected, the intellect is purified, and the will is merged into the Cosmic Will. That is, it is no longer centered upon narrow personal ends, but is concerned with the good of all.

A man is not wholly victorious until he is perpetually calm. While passing things disturb him, his understanding is unripe, his heart is not altogether pure. A man cannot advance in the triumph of life while he flatters and deceives himself. He must awake, and be fully alive to the fact that his sins, sorrows, and troubles are of his own making, and belong to his own imperfect condition. He must understand that his miseries have their root in his own sins, and not in the sins of others. He must strive after calmness as the covetous man strives after riches; and he must not rest satisfied with any partial attainment. He will thus grow in grace and wisdom, in strength and peace, and calmness will descend upon his spirit as the refreshing dew descends upon the flowers.

Where the calm mind is, there is strength and rest, there is love and wisdom. There is one who has fought successfully innumerable battles against self, who, after long toil in secret against his own failings, has triumphed at last.

Insight and Nobility

IN THE PURSUIT AND PRACTICE OF VIRTUE, there at last comes a time when a divine insight dawns upon the mind. It searches into the causes and principles of things, which, once attained, establishes its possessor firmly in virtue. It renders him invulnerable to the assaults of temptation, and invincible in his work for the world.

When the understanding is ripened by the culture of virtue, vicious inclinations disappear, and wrong-doing becomes impossible. When individual conduct is perceived as an unbroken series of causes and effects, the perceiving mind finally decides for virtue, and the lower selfish elements are just cast away forever.

Until a man perceives the just law which operates in human life, whatever virtue he may manifest at any given time, he is not firmly established in nobility of character, he is not fully armored with righteousness, and is not safely lodged in his final refuge. Not having acquired that perfect insight which knows good and evil and which perceives the effects of all deeds both good and bad, he breaks down when assailed by temptation at those points in his character which are not well fortified. Those which have, so far, dimmed his spiritual insight, and barred him from perfect vision. By thus breaking down, he discovers that within which has hindered him. And by setting to work to remove the hindrance, he ascends still higher in the scale of virtue, and approaches nearer to the perfect insight into the true order of life which makes a man divine.

Under certain circumstances a man, held in restraint by the influence of friends, by custom and environment, and not by his own inherent purity and strength, will appear to have, and may believe he possesses, a virtue of which he knows nothing in reality. And his lack of such virtue only appears when all outward restraints are withdrawn, and, under temptation, the concealed weakness and vice make themselves manifest.

On the other hand, the man of superior virtue will seem, in a familiar environment, to be much the same as his weaker fellows, and his virtue will not be apparent to those about him. But when he is suddenly brought in contact with great temptations or extraordinary events, his latent virtue appears in all its beauty and strength.

The Root of Evil is Ignorance

Insight destroys the dominion of evil and reveals the faultless operation of the Good Law. The man of perfect insight cannot sin, because he fully understands the nature of good and evil. And it is impossible for one who knows good and evil, in all their ramifications of cause and effect, to choose the evil and reject the good. Just as the sane man would not choose ashes in preference to food, so the spiritually awakened man would not choose evil in preference to good. The presence of sin is an indication of self-delusion and of ignorance; the spiritual vision is warped or undeveloped, and there is confusion of mind concerning the nature of good and evil.

In the early stages of virtue, a man arrays himself against the forces of evil which appear to him to be overpowering in their might, and almost, if not entirely, unconquerable. But with the advent of insight, a new light is thrown upon the nature of things, and evil appears as it actually is—a small, dark, powerless thing, a mere negation, and not a formidable force or combination of forces. The man of insight knows that the root of evil is ignorance—and not an intelligent power—and that all sin and suffering proceed therefrom. Thus, knowing evil to be merely a depravation of good, he cannot hate it, but manifests compassion for all sinning and suffering beings.

Reaching the Divine Goodness

Indeed, he who has so far conquered the evil in his own heart, as to know the nature and source of evil, cannot possibly hate, dislike, or despise any being, no matter how far removed from virtue it may be. But, while fully perceiving the degradation of character, he understands the dark spiritual condition from which such degradation springs, and so he pities and helps where, without insight, he would hate and despise. Love ever attends upon insight, and pity waits on knowledge.

That insight which proceeds from self-purification and long acquaintance with virtue makes itself manifest in the form of ripeness of character. There is an unchanging strength and sweetness combined; a clearness of intellect, a virile strength of will and a gentleness of heart—a combination which denotes a cultured, mellowed, perfected being; one who has acquired sympathy, compassion, purity, and wisdom. Thus, while "Goodness gives insight," insight renders goodness permanent, fixes the mind in the love and practice of all that is pure and noble, and stamps upon man's brow the seal of divinity.

The man whose goodness is of the kind that does not alter with altered environment, or with the changing attitudes of those around him, has reached the Divine Goodness; he understands the Supreme Good. He is no longer concerned with evil as a thing that can harm, but he is concerned with good only. And so he ignores evil and recognizes only good. He perceives that men commit evil out of the mistaken idea of good, and, thus perceiving, no hatred against any can enter his peaceful heart.

The life of such a man is powerful, no matter how obscure it may be, for goodness is the most powerful thing in the world. The fact of his living and moving among men confers incalculable benefit upon the race, although during his lifetime this may not be perceived or understood. So powerful is goodness that the destiny of the world was, is, and will be in the hands of the good.

The Emancipators of Humankind

Those who are good are the guides and emancipators of humanity. In the present period of its development, they are taking the race rapidly along in its evolutionary journey; and this, not in any mystical or miraculous sense, but in a very practical and normal sense, by their exemplary lives, by the power of their deeds. The good men who help the world are not wonder-workers, though undeveloped minds have ever tried to make them such—but the workers of righteousness, servants of the Good Law.

The world never was, is not, and will not be, under the dominion of evil, for such a condition would mean non-existence, evil being merely the negation of good, as darkness is the negation of light. It is light, and not darkness which is the sustaining power. Evil is the weakest thing in the world, and cannot accomplish anything. The universe not only makes for good, the universe is good, and evil always falls short and fails.

The Truth About Insight

Insight is seeing in the Light of Truth, that Light which is the revealer of all things. As the light of day reveals all objects in the world in their proper forms, so when the Light of Truth enters the mind it reveals all the things of life in their proper proportions. He who searches his own heart by the aid of Truth, searches all hearts. He who, by long searching, has perceived the Perfect Law which is operative in his mind, has revealed the Divine Law which is the stay and substance of the universe.

Insight disperses error and puts an end to superstition. Sin is the only error. Men attack each other's beliefs and remain in ignorance. When they get rid of their own sins they will become enlightened. Superstition springs from sin. Looking through darkened eyes, men see evil things which are delusions of ignorance; conceiving in their hearts unlawful things, their imagination is troubled with monsters and terrors which have no existence in reality. Where there is pure insight there is no fear. Devils, demons, wrathful and jealous gods, vampires and evil spirits, and all the hideous host of the ideological monsters, have vanished from the universe along with the feverish nightmare which gave them birth. And before the rapt gaze of the purified one there spreads a universe of orderly beauty and inviolate law.

Saintliness is a Normal Condition of Mind

The man of insight lives in the beatific vision of the saints, not as a fleeting experience in a moment of exceptional purity, but as a constant, normal condition of mind. He has completed his long journey through self and sorrow, and is at peace. He has conquered, and is glad.

He sees all the sin, misery, and pain that are in the world more plainly and vividly than other men. But he now sees it as it is in its cause, inception, growth, and fruitage, not as it appeared to him when he was blindly involved in it, and his mind was distorted by impurities.

He watches the growth of beings, from the immature to the mature, through periods of change and pain, with tender compassion and solicitude, as the mother watches the growth of her child through the helpless period of its infancy.

He sees justice operating in all things. While men are waxing wrathful over the triumph of wrong, he knows that wrong has not triumphed, but is brought to naught. He sees the overruling Right which, though concealed from worldly eyes, remains forever unshaken. He sees the littleness, the puny weakness, the blind folly of evil as compared with the majesty, the invincible power, and the all-seeing wisdom of Good. And thus, knowing and seeing, his mind is finally fixed in that which is good. He is devoted to Truth, and his delight is in the doing of righteousness.

The Triumph of Good

When insight is born in the mind, Reality stands revealed; not a metaphysical reality distinct from the universe; not a speculative reality other than the things of life, but the Reality of the universe itself, the Reality of "things-in-themselves." Insight is triumphant over change and decay, for it perceives the abiding in change, the eternal in the transient, the immortal in the things which pass away.

And herein is the meaning of that fixed nobility of character of the saints and sages, and superlatively, of the Great Teachers of the Race—that they perceive and abide in Reality. They know life in its completion; they understand and obey the Righteous Law. Having conquered self, they have conquered all delusions; have triumphed over sin, they have triumphed over sorrow; having purified themselves, they see the Perfect Cosmos.

He who chooses the right, the pure, the good, and clings to them through all misunderstandings, insults, and defeat, reaches, at last, the place of insight, and his eyes open upon the world of truth. Then his painful discipline is ended; the lower conditions no more affect him or cause him sorrow. Purity and joy abide with him, and the universe again rejoices in the triumph of good, and hails another conqueror.

Man the Master

By the mastery of self, a distinct form of consciousness is evolved which some would call divine. It is distinguished from that ordinary human consciousness, which craves personal advantages and gratifications on the one hand, and is involved in remorse and sorrow on the other. This divine consciousness concerns itself with humanity and the universe, with eternal verities, with righteousness, wisdom, and truth, and not with pleasures, protection, and preservation of the personality. Not that personal pleasure is destroyed, but that it is no longer craved and sought, it no longer takes a foremost place. It is purified, and it is received as the effect of right thought and action. and is no longer an end in itself.

Divine Consciousness and Self-Consciousness

In divine consciousness there is neither sin nor

sorrow. Even the sense of sin has passed away, and the true order and purpose of life being revealed, no cause is found for lamentation. Jesus called this state of consciousness "The Kingdom of Heaven"; Buddha named it "Nirvana"; Lao-Tze's term for it was "Tao"; Emerson refers to it as "The Over-Soul"; and Dr. Bucke calls it "Cosmic Consciousness" in his valuable work bearing that title.

The ordinary human consciousness is self-consciousness. Self, the personality, is placed before everything else. There are ceaseless anxieties and fears concerning the self. Its possible loss is thought to be the most grievous calamity, and its eternal preservation the most important thing in the universe.

In divine consciousness all this has passed away. Self has disappeared. Therefore, there can be no more fears and anxieties concerning the self, and things are considered and known as they are, and not as they afford pleasure or cause pain to self, not as self wishes them to be for its own temporal or eternal happiness.

The self-conscious man is subject to desire; the divinely conscious man is master of desire. The former considers what is pleasant or unpleasant; the latter acts from the righteous law without reference to pleasure or pain.

The Great Teachers

The race is passing through self-consciousness to divine consciousness; through the slavery of self, with its sense of sin and shame, to the freedom of Truth, with its sense of purity and power. The Great Teachers and Saviors of the race have already attained. In former existences they have already passed through all forms of self-consciousness, and now, having subjugated self, have become divinely conscious.

They have reached the summit of evolution on this earth, and have no further need to be reborn in the self-conscious form. They are Masters of Life. Having conquered self, they have acquired the Supreme Knowledge. Some of them are worshiped as God because they manifest a wisdom and a consciousness which is quite distinct from the normal self-consciousness of humanity, and which is therefore regarded with, and surrounded by, incomprehensible mystery. Yet, in this divine consciousness there is no mystery, but, on the contrary, a transparent simplicity which becomes apparent when the confusions of self are dispersed.

The abiding gentleness, the sublime wisdom, the perfect calm of the Great Teachers—qualities which appear supernatural when viewed from the self-consciousness state—are seen to be simple and natural when the first glimmering of divine consciousness dawns in the mind. And such divine consciousness does not appear until a high degree of morality is attained by self-conscious man.

The Master and the Slave

Man becomes divinely conscious, divinely wise, divinely gentle and strong in the measure that he subdues and dominates within, those passions by which humanity is subdued and dominated. The divine master is one who has attained mastery over self. The abiding nobility, beneficent characteristics, and unobtrusive virtue which mark off the spiritually enlightened man from others, are the fruits of self-conquest, the logical outcome of a long struggle to master and comprehend those mental forces which the self-conscious man blindly obeys without understanding.

Self-conscious man is a slave to self. Obeying self-centered inclinations, he is in submission to his passions, and to the sorrows and pains which allegiance to those passions inflict upon him. He is conscious of sin and sorrow, but sees no way out of these conditions. And so he invents theologies which he substitutes for effort, and which, while affording him fitful comfort through uncertain hope, leave him the easy victim of sin, and the willing prey of sorrow.

Divinely conscious man is the master of self. He obeys Truth and not self. He curbs and directs his inclinations and is conscious of a growing power over sin and sorrow. He sees that there is a way out of these conditions by the path of self-mastery. He needs no theologies to aid him, but exerts himself in right-doing, and is gladdened by a sense of victory and increasing purity and power. When his mastery is complete, he has no inclinations but those which accord with Truth. He has then become the conqueror of sin, and is no longer subject to sorrow.

Enlightened, wise, and evermore peaceful and happy is he who has subjected, overcome, and cast out the turbulent self that reigned within. The tempests of sorrow do not chill him. The cares and troubles which beset man pass him by, and no evil thing overtakes him. Secure in divine virtue, no enemy can overthrow him; no foe can do harm. Kind and peaceful, no person, power, nor place can rob him of repose.

The Worst Enemy is Self

There is no enemy but self, no darkness but ignorance, no suffering but that which springs from the insubordinate elements of one's own nature.

No man is truly wise who is involved in likes and dislikes, wishes and regrets, desires and disappointments, sins and sorrow. All these conditions belong to the self-conscious state, and are indications of folly, weakness, and subjection.

He is truly wise who, in the midst of worldly duties, is always calm, always gentle, always patient. He accepts things as they are, and does not wish nor grieve, desire nor regret. These things belong to the divinely conscious state, the dominion of Truth, and are indications of enlightenment, strength, and mastery.

He who does not desire riches, fame, or pleasures; who enjoys what he has, yet does not lament when it is taken from him, he is indeed wise.

He who desires riches, fame, and pleasure; who is discontented with what he has, yet laments when it is taken from him, he is indeed foolish.

Destined for Mastery

Man is fitted for conquest, but the conquest of territory will not avail; he must resort to the conquest of self. The conquest of territory renders man a temporal ruler, but the conquest of self makes him an eternal conqueror.

Man is destined for mastery; not the mastery of

his fellow men by force, but the mastery of his own nature by self-control. The mastery of his fellow men by force is the crown of egotism, but the mastery of self by self-control is the crown of humility.

He is man the master who has shaken off the service of self for the service of Truth, who has established himself in the Eternal Verities. He is crowned, not only with perfect manhood, but with divine wisdom. He has overcome the disturbances of the mind and the shocks of life. He is superior to all circumstances. He is the calm spectator, but no longer the helpless tool, of events. No more a sinning, weeping, repenting mortal, he is pure, rejoicing, upright immortal. He perceives the course of things with a glad and peaceful heart; a divine conqueror, master of life and death.

Knowledge and Victory

FAITH IS THE BEGINNING of the Triumphant Life, but knowledge is its consummation. Faith reveals the way, but knowledge is the goal. Faith suffers many afflictions; knowledge has transcended affliction. Faith endures; knowledge loves. Faith walks in darkness, but believes; knowledge acts in light, and knows. Faith inspires to effort; knowledge crowns effort with success. "Faith is the substance of things hoped for"; knowledge is the substance of those things possessed. Faith is the helpful staff of the pilgrim; knowledge is the City of Refuge at the journey's end. Without faith there will be no knowledge, but when knowledge is acquired, the work of faith is finished.

The Life Triumphant is a life of knowledge; and by knowledge is meant, not book-learning, but life-learning; not superficial facts committed to memory, but the deep facts and truths of life, grasped and comprehended. Apart from this knowledge there is no victory for man, no rest for his weary feet, no refuge for his aching heart.

Knowledge is Salvation

There is no salvation for the foolish except by becoming wise. There is no salvation for the sinful except by becoming pure. There is no liberation for man from the turmoil and troubles of life but through divine knowledge reached by the pathway of a pure and blameless life. Nowhere is there permanent peace except in an enlightened condition of mind; and a pure life and an enlightened mind are identical.

But there is salvation for the foolish because wisdom can be acquired. There is salvation for the sinful because purity can be embraced. There is liberation for all men from the troubles and turmoil of life because whosoever wills to do so—whether rich or poor, learned or unlearned—can enter the lowly way of blamelessness which leads to perfect knowledge. And because of this—that there is deliverance for the captives and victory for the defeated—there is rejoicing in the High Places, and the universe is glad.

The man of knowledge, being victorious over himself, is victorious over sin, over evil, over all the disharmonies of life. Out of the old mind marred by sin and sorrow, he has framed a new mind glorified by purity and peace. He has died out of the old world of evil, and is reborn in a new world where love and faultless law prevail, where evil is not, and he has become deathless in immortal Good.

The Wise are Free from Sorrow

Anxiety and fear, grief and lamentation, disappointment and regret, wretchedness and remorse—these things have no part in the world of the wise. They are the shadowy inhabitants of the world of self, and cannot live, nay, they are seen to have no substantiality—in the light of wisdom. The dark things of life are the dark conditions of a mind not yet illuminated by the light of wisdom. They follow self as the shadow of substance. Where selfish desires go, there they follow; where sin is, there they are. There is no rest in self; there is no light in self. And where the flames of turbulent passions and fires of consuming desires are rife, the cool airs of wisdom and peace are not felt.

Safety and assurance, happiness and repose, satisfaction and contentment, joy and peace—these are the abiding possessions of the wise, earned by right of self-conquest, the results of righteousness, the wages of a blameless life.

The substance of a right life is enlightenment (knowledge), and the spirit of knowledge is peace. To be victorious over self in all the issues of life is to know life as it is in reality, and not as it appears in the nightmare of self. It is to be in peace in all passages, and not to be stricken with trouble and grief in the common happenings of life.

As the ripe scholar is no more troubled by incorrect work and lessons imperfectly done, and the painful reproof and punishment formerly inflicted by his teachers are left behind forever, so the perfected scholar in virtue, the wise man and woman, the enlightened doer of righteousness, is no more troubled with wrongdoing and folly (which are merely the imperfectly accomplished lessons of life), and the scourging of sorrow and remorse have passed away forever.

The skilled scholar has no more doubt or fear concerning his ability. He has overcome and dispersed the ignorance of his intellect. He has attained to learning, and he knows that he has attained. And he so knows because, having undergone innumerable tests in the forms of lessons and examinations, he has at last proved his skill by passing successfully through the severest tests of scholarship. And now he no longer fears, but rejoices when severe tests are applied to prove his ability. He is capable, confident, and glad.

Even so the skilled doer of righteousness is no more troubled with doubt and fear concerning his destiny. He has overcome and dispersed the ignorance of his heart. He has attained to wisdom, and he knows that he has attained. And he so knows because where he formerly failed and fell when tested by the wrong conduct of others, he now maintains his patience and calmness under the severest tests of accusation and reproof.

Herein is the glory and victory of divine knowledge, that understanding the nature of deeds, both good and bad, the enlightened doer of good deeds no longer suffers through the bad deeds of others. Their actions towards him can never cause him pain and sorrow, nor rob him of his peace. Having taken refuge in good, evil can no more reach nor harm him. He returns good for evil, and overcomes the weakness of evil by the power of good.

Arise and Ascend to Your Throne

The man who is involved in bad deeds imagines that the bad deeds of others are powerful to do him injury and are filled with grievous harm against him. He is stung with pain and overwhelmed with sorrow, not for his own bad deeds (for these he does not see) but for the wrong deeds of others. Involved in ignorance, he has no spiritual strength, no refuge, and no abiding peace.

The man victorious over self is the true seer. He is not the seer of spirits or supernatural phenomena, for such seeing is narrow and illusory. He is the seer of life as it is, both in its particular aspects and in its divine principles; the seer of the spiritual universe of cosmic law, cosmic love, and cosmic liberty.

The man of knowledge and victory, who has shaken off the painful dreams of self, has awakened with a new vision which beholds a new and glorified universe. He is the seer of the Eternal, and is blessed with perfect love and endless peace. He is lifted far above all sordid desires, narrow aims, and selfish love and hate; and being so lifted up he perceives the lawful course of things, and does not grieve when overtaken by the inevitable. He is above the world of sorrow, not because he has become cold and cruel, but because he abides in a love where no thought of self can enter, and where the well-being of others is all-in-all. He is sorrowless because he is selfless. He is serene because he knows that whatever he receives, it is good, and whatever is taken from him, that also is good. He has transmuted sorrow into love, and is filled with infinite tenderness and abounding compassion. His power is not violent, ambitious, worldly, but pure, peaceful, heavenly, and he is possessed of a hidden strength which knows how to stand and when to bend for the good of others and the world.

He is a Teacher, though he speaks but little. He is a Master, yet he has no desire to rule others. He is a Conqueror, but makes no attempt to subdue his fellow men. He has become a conscious instrument for the outworking of cosmic law, and is an intelligent, enlightened power directing the evolution of the Race.

At this, the beginning of a new epoch, let the Good News again go forth throughout the world that there is purity for the sinful, comfort for the afflicted, healing for the broken-hearted, and triumph for the defeated. In your heart, O man! O woman! stained as it is with sin, and torn with conflicting desires, there is a place of power, a citadel of strength. You are the dwelling-place of the Supreme Good, and the Scepter of Victory awaits you: deep in your consciousness is the High Seat of Empire. Arise, O stricken one! Ascend your rightly throne!

More Titles in the James Allen Wisdom Series

The Wisdom of James Allen

5 Classic Works Combined into One

by James Allen Edited by Andy Zubko

Softcover 384 pp. $9.95 ISBN: 1-889606-00-6

For over a hundred years, James Allen's best-known work, *As a Man Thinketh,* has inspired thousands of readers to live more successful and effective lives. *The Wisdom of James Allen* contains *As a Man Thinketh* with four more of his classic works: *The Path to Prosperity*, *The Mastery of Destiny*, *The Way of Peace*, and *Entering the Kingdom.*

EXCERPT FROM *WISDOM OF JAMES ALLEN*:

The greatest achievement was at first and for a time a dream. The oak sleeps in the acorn; the bird sleeps in the egg; and in the highest vision of the soul a waking angel stirs. Dreams are the seedlings of realities....

Your circumstances may be uncongenial, but they shall not long remain so if you but perceive an Ideal and strive to reach it. You cannot travel within and stand still without....Whatever your present environment may be, you will fall, remain, or rise with your thoughts, your Vision, your Ideal. You will become as small as your controlling desire; as great as your dominant aspiration. —From *As a Man Thinketh*

More Titles in the James Allen Wisdom Series

The Wisdom of James Allen III

4 Classic Works from the author of

As a Man Thinketh

by James Allen Edited by Andy Zubko

Softcover 352pp. $10.95 ISBN: 1-889606-08-1

The Wisdom of James Allen III is the third volume in the Laurel Creek James Allen Wisdom Series. It combines 4 more classic James Allen works including: *Out from the Heart*, *Byways of Blessedness*, *From Passion to Peace*, and *The Heavenly Life*.

Excerpt from *Wisdom of James Allen III*

As the heart, so is the life. The within is ceaselessly becoming the without. Nothing remains unrevealed. That which is hidden is but for a time, it ripens and comes forth at last. Seed, tree, blossom, and fruit are the fourfold order of the universe. From the state of your heart proceeds the conditions of your life. Your thoughts blossom into deeds; and your deeds bear the fruitage of character and destiny....Life is ever unfolding from within and revealing itself to the light, and thoughts engendered in the heart at last reveal themselves in words, actions, and things accomplished. As the fountain from the hidden spring, so flows forth your life from the secret recesses of your heart. —From *Out from the Heart*